Advanced Airbrush Art

How to Secrets from the Masters

Timothy Remus

Published by:
Wolfgang Publications Inc.
217 Second Street North
Stillwater, MN 55082
http://www.wolfpub.com

Legals

First published in 2005 by Wolfgang Publications Inc.,
217 Second Street North, Stillwater MN 55082

The information in this book is true and complete to the best of our
knowledge. All recommendations are made without any guarantee
on the part of the author or publisher, who also disclaim any liabili-
ty incurred in connection with the use of this data or specific details.

We recognize that some words, model names and designations, for
example, mentioned herein are the property of the trademark holder.
We use them for identification purposes only. This is not an official
publication.

ISBN number: 1-929133-20-0

Printed and bound in Canada

Advanced Airbursh Art

Acknowledgements

As I've explained elsewhere in this book, what you hold in your hands is a series of start-to-finish sequences, shot in the shops of various well-known airbrush artists. Thus the first ones to thank are the artists themselves.

Let me start by extending my thanks to Andy Anderson, who photographed his own sequence and then wrote the copy. A few more artists like Andy and I could give up working Saturdays.

In the case of Chris Cruz, I was hoping to shoot a mural, but ended up documenting a graphic instead. Which may be a good thing as it reinforces the full range of Chris' talent.

Working with Vince Goodeve meant a journey all the way to the great white north. But the weather wasn't too bad and the hospitality more than made up for any chill in the air.

And though our offices are in the same metro area, there's enough freeway between Leah and Brian Gall's barn and my office that I seldom see the dynamic duo. The book was a chance to spend a little time together and reacquaint myself with their synergistic talents.

The same could be said for Lenni Schwartz, who lives only about fifteen miles from my office. I often see Lenni's designs on a new Donnie Smith bike, but seldom have the pleasure of watching one of Lenni's images develop from sketch to finished paint.

When I showed up at Keith Hanson's shop for a week of photography, he had just suffered a personal loss. Being a professional however, Keith re-grouped about three days later and put down a great Keith-Hanson graphic on a Dave Perewitz machine.

John Nicholas was doing very manual labor when he was "discovered" and convinced to come to work as an airbrush artist at the K.C. Creations paint shop. Life is seldom fair, but in this case it was and a man with tremendous ability and a slim portfolio got a change to develop both his talent and his portfolio.

Nick Pastura not only let me into his shop, but into his house and life as well. Here is a man with a wide range of abilities, and a great assortment of very good cigars.

Documenting the work of Steve Wizard meant going all the way to Ohio, but the trip was definitely worth it. The eagle and reality flames graphic is simply one very over-the-top design that I'm pleased to have in this book.

Slow is how Matt Willoughby describes himself. His humility is sincere, a word that pretty much describes Matt, except for a few others like: creative, hard working and accomplished.

To one and all I offer up my thanks. Thanks for allowing me into your lives, for putting up with my intrusive camera, for sharing your secrets and mostly, for letting me witness first hand the magic that is art.

This book required considerable travel and I would be remiss if I didn't thank my various hosts, including Big Rick, Lou from Ohio, Paul and Karen Shadley, and Kim and Cheryl Suter.

Thanks to Krista Leary for keeping our little office running, and to Jacki Mitchell for the fine layout. Final thanks go to my lovely and talented wife, Mary Lanz, who makes it all possible.

Introduction

During the roughly fifteen years I've been cranking out how-to books, it's been my good fortune to encounter some very talented painters. From custom painters like Jon Kosmoski to airbrush artists like Nancy Brooks, I'm always impressed with the colors, the quality, the drive for perfection and the sheer imagination. Each of my book projects seems to beget another, and past books with aforementioned artists (and others) begot this one.

The idea was (is) to build an airbrush book based not just on how-to techniques or the latest and best airbrushes, but on the artists themselves. I've left out airbrushing 101 and the section that covers the chemistry of urethane basecoats. This book is a series of real - life, hands-on sequences photographed in each artists' shop. From page 6 to page 141, this book is photo sequences and short interviews. As much as possible I've tried to get out of the way, to let each artist, and each set of photographs, tell the story.

And the stories range from skulls to graphics, from reality flames to pin-ups. Some of the projects cover all of the above. The real story is the way the various artists do what they do best: How Andy Anderson creates a tapered shadow so the spear he painted appears to rise up above the rest of the paint job. Why Vince Goodeve likes to use complimentary colors in his designs. The way Matt Willoughby uses a mechanical pen to create detail that's almost too small to see.

Most of the information is conveyed in the projects themselves. In the subtle differences in shading that occur as Leah Gall creates a very realistic human form, in the way a Keith Hanson graphic develops, in the sequence of colors Steve Wizard uses to create reality flames, in the way John Nicholas makes the spilled whiskey run out of the bottle and then catch fire.

The rest of the information comes through the interviews, called Q&A in this case. Perhaps my favorite part of the book, this is a chance to learn first-hand how Chris Cruz makes murals you can walk into, or share Nick Pastura's tricks for painting designs and lettering on helmets.

The information is here, it's up to you to put it to good use.

Chapter One

Vince Goodeve

Multiple Skulls & 3-D Graphics

Documented here is the work of Vince Goodeve, well-known airbrush artist from Owen Sound, Ontario, and VQ Magazine's Painter of the Year for 2001. Vince is an airbrush artist known for the incredible detail that sets his work apart from all others. The work documented here might be called two part and includes both a graphic done on the side of the tank, and a mural of skulls running the length of the tank.

The first photos show the tank with a base-

The harmony of color and balance of darks in the graphic, as well as the imagery on top, is the key to a relatively simple, but clean and attractive, paint scheme.

coat, and the underlying swirl of pearl. To create the swirl Vince used spray mask, a spray-able masking solution (Spray-lat is the company that makes this "sign stripe blue" product). This water-based product needs to be sprayed on and left to dry overnight. As Vince explains, "once it was dry I drew the ellipses with a sharpie, cut that out with an Xacto knife and sprayed the yellow pearl over the orange pearl base. The base paint is PPG metallic orange, the yellow base is a custom mix of PPG toners. Once the yellow dried I just peeled off the spray mask. Though it's made for masking out sections of signs this is an excellent product for round or curved surfaces. You do have to make sure you apply it correctly (thick enough) though or you'll never get it off." (Before applying any masking materials Vince puts down two coats of lockdown clear, PPG 895, to protect the basecoat.)

With the swirl finished Vince starts with a sketch of the graphic, which was scanned into the computer, sized to fit the tank and then cut out by the plotter/cutter. The plotter uses low-tack vinyl so it won't leave behind any residue.

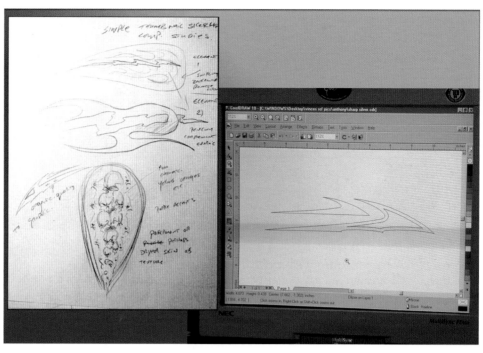

The design for the graphic used on the sides of the tank starts as a sketch, which Vince scans into the computer.

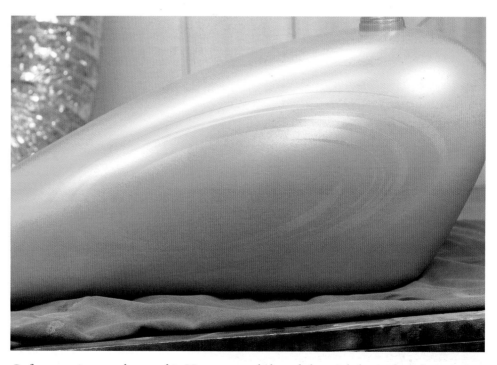

Before starting on the graphic Vince created the subtle swirl shown here by spraying the tank with masking solution (sign stripe blue), then cutting out the ellipses, and finally painting with yellow pearl over the orange pearl base.

Note: Our 6-panel pages are constructed in columns - they start on the top left, read down to the bottom, then across to the top right and down again.

The graphic is already done on the left side, because the design was scanned into the computer it's easy to cut out a duplicate for the other side of the tank.

Now the mask can be pulled off the backing paper…

Application tape is applied to the design, this will make it easier to pick up the cut-out and apply it to the tank…

…before being applied to the tank.

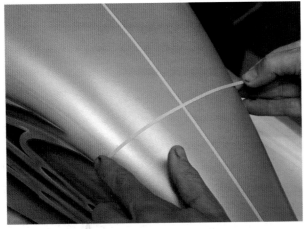

…but before applying the mask it's important to measure from the centerline so the two designs are in exactly the same position.

Bubbles are worked out first by hand, and then with a squeegee.

As shown, Vince puts application tape over the top of the mask before he peels off the backing. Next the mask is positioned carefully to match the work already done on the other side of the tank and all the bubbles are worked out with a squeegee.

Vince starts painting with transparent red, mixed with just a little transparent purple, both from the Global PPG mixing system. "I like to use transparent toners," explains Vince. "I seldom use candy, except sometimes the KK line from House of Kolor. These PPG toners are like a basecoat."

"You have to have a good steady hand. This is just like using a candy on a paint job. I put more coats down on the bottom to create a shadow. With the bottom done I do a very light coat on the top, I use the same stroke and trigger pull, but I move the gun farther back from the surface. For this I'm using medium-speed reducer, (2 parts reducer to 1 part paint). The paint is red (D-745) and violet (D-755), mixed 90% red, 10% violet. And I have the regulator set at 35 psi. For graphics I like to use bottles on an Iwata Eclipse airbrush. It's a middle of the road airbrush and it gives pretty good detail. The parts are cheaper for these than they are for a more expensive gun. At this point I include a few dagger strokes to add punch, but you have to be careful that you don't overdo it."

Now the application paper can be pulled off…

…, leaving only the mask behind.

Let the painting begin, with transparent red in this case. "You don't have to hog this paint on too heavy, better to come in with a darker color later…"

"…rather than build up transparent color real deep, this way there's less milage at the edge. It makes the clearcoating easier."

The next step is to apply violet to the top of the red stripe. The idea is to darken the red without loosing the fade on the bottom of the red.

"In this series I make 4 passes to get the tone that I want. You have to do it the same on all parts of the design."

"I like a 2 handed approach, my upper body and shoulders are all part of it."

Next I do a light overcoat, holding the airbrush farther back from the tank, just to be sure the color is consistent and balanced.

"I use passion purple from H of K at the transition on the very bottom of the red/purple areas which creates a nice pinky-orange blend into the orange."

The next color is Violet, (D 755). This is mixed 2 parts medium speed reducer and 1 part paint. "Reduce the paint so that at 35 psi it atomizes nicely," explains Vince, "instead of giving you that rough spattery look. I always do a test spray, each time I change paint."

"On the red at the bottom I hit the top of the stripe to darken the red using nice even strokes. If I use purple straight onto orange it would just turn ugly brown, so we had to put down the red first. The idea is to avoid a big build up of paint at the edge where you're going to pull the mask off. The imaginary light source is on the top, all the shadows are consistent with that illusion."

Now Vince masks off the area where he doesn't want the effect of the loose mask. Purple is the color Vince sprays through the loose mask, he sprays an even pattern for even coverage. Next, he darkens the shadow a bit more and pulls the green

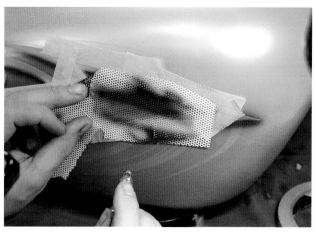

I'm always looking for what I call loose masks to create texture and complexity. This mask creates a mesh-like pattern. The color used here is purple.

The tape is pulled and the mask is moved to other parts of the graphic.

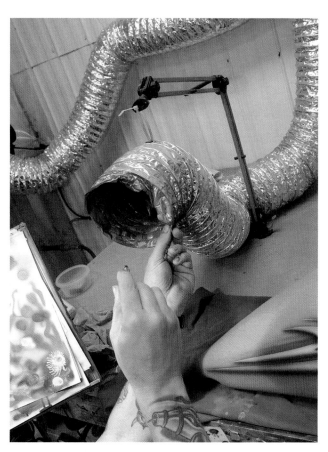

After every paint change it's important to test the pattern and make sure the airbrush isn't spitting. This exhaust system is nice because it's movable.

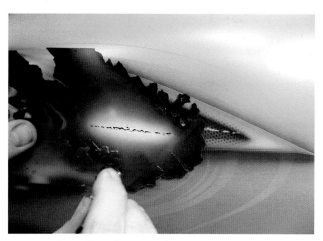

A second mask and some white paint are used to create a broken line through the center of the pattern painted earlier.

11

"To knock the white back toward the purple side I hit it with a little transparent purple, (D-755)."

The paint being used on the edge is the transparent red used earlier, with 5% purple.

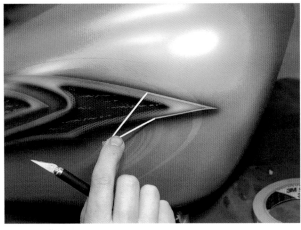

To create a beveled edge Vince first pulls the outer edge of the tape.

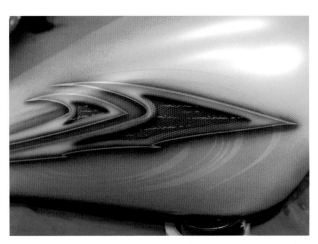

This shows the graphic after a slight mist of red over the newly exposed bevel area.

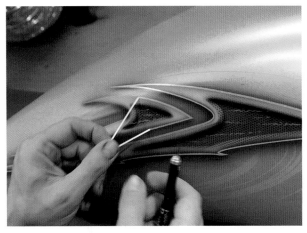

"The idea is to enhance this edge so it steps away from the main graphic body."

"A simple mask is my tool of choice to create the effect of a shadow."

masking tape. To create the broken line done in off-white Vince uses another mask. Then, "to tone down the white I hit it with the transparent purple to knock it back toward the purple side."

Now we are going to remove the outer trim from the mask, (this will be the bevel). This thin section was cut on the plotter earlier, but not pulled off until now. The idea is to enhance this area so it steps away from the main graphic body. For this area Vince is using transparent red with 5% purple, (the first color).

"I always spray the paint onto a scrap of paper before spraying the object," explains Vince, "so you know the airbrush won't spit on the object I'm painting. This is a very subtle effect, it doesn't take much to create the effect I'm after. Now I use a mask to create the suggestion of a shadow, a shadow that indicates there's a beveled edge."

Next, Vince pulls off the big part of the mask, explaining as he does, "you have to make sure the two sides of the tank are the same at this point and make any small adjustments necessary to achieve that."

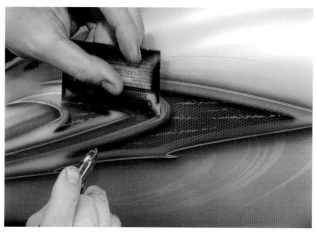

As the mask is lifted up you can see the subtle effect that defines the beveled edge.

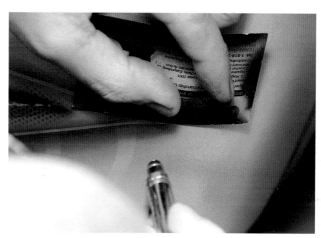

The beveled shadows are sprayed on each of the corners.

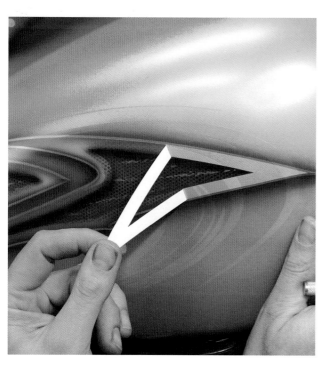

Pulling the mask is done slowly to minimize pulling any paint.

Now it's time to pull the biggest part of the mask.

13

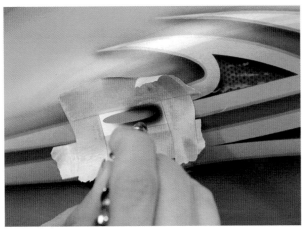

Four small ellipses are added next, with the help of a small mask. The mask is used primarily for the front of the ellipse…

"Here I'm adding highlights, which reinforces the light source and direction, but I'm staying off the bevel I created earlier."

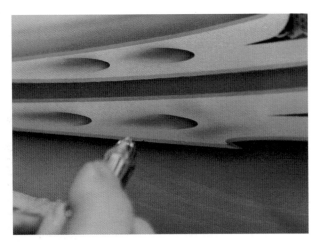

…the back and highlights are done by hand

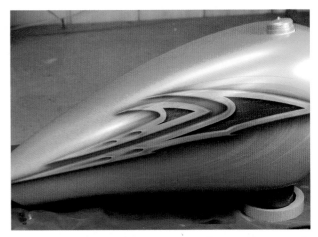

"The finished graphic has a nice flow, and it's made up of complimentary colors like orange and purple so it's a more harmonious piece."

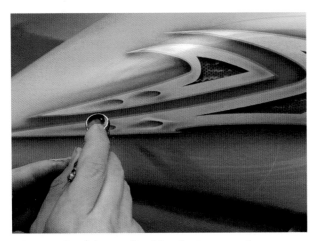

"For really tight work I like the Micron, but you have to buy the "C" model with solvent-resistant O-rings.

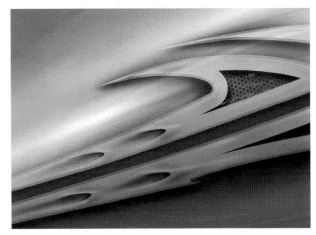

Details show how everything works together. Hard edges, soft flowing color transitions, as well as textures and movement.

ELLIPTICAL HIGHLIGHTS

The small ellipses are added at this point. The main part of each is created with a mask that Vince cuts by hand. First he does the front edge of the small ellipse, for this edge he applies a heavier application of paint.. The back part of each ellipse is done free-hand. "Now I add a little color to the main part of the design, but lightly, because I want it to look transparent."

At this point Vince switches to a different gun, one of the Iwata microns, for more control. "I add slow reducer to my mix right now," explains Vince, "so it won't dry too fast. When you're doing detail work the paint can dry on the tip, you need to slow down the evaporation. I'm adding highlights to the tops of the small ellipses. Again, this suggests the light source. I build them up slowly, and I stay off the bevel so I don't destroy that line I created."

"I'm using pure toner from PPG (DMX 210), part of the Radiance line. This is what they make candy from. I can use it without hiding any of the detail, but you have to use it sparingly, this stuff is strong. What I like about it is it's so transparent. I use it straight, 2 parts red, 1 part medium-speed reducer. It richens the paint I put down earlier.

THE MURAL

Before starting on the mural Vince draws a center line on the tank and then sketches the skulls out with pencil (see the top of page 15). "I don't put down too much detail when I sketch on the tank like this," explains Vince. "because then you're married to the sketch. And you have to cover each of the lines you draw, so it's better to keep the sketch pretty loose. I'm careful to avoid getting oils from my hand on the tank. Anyplace I rest my hand on the tank I wipe off with wax and grease remover. If I don't, there will be a problem later.

Vince uses the same colors on the mural that were used on the side panels, but knocked down a little more. "The most important thing about painting a mural with tight detail is your paint mixture, you want it thick enough to cover and achieve image, but not so thick it dries on the tip or spits. This is where slow reducer comes in

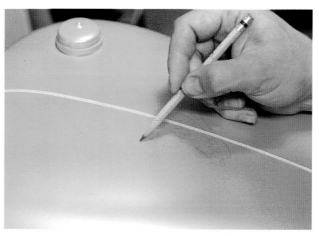

After pulling tape down the centerline of the tank, Vince does a "pretty loose" sketch of the skulls directly on the paint.

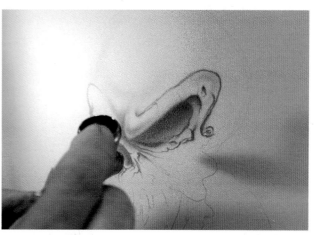

Vince is using almost the same colors here, the same red with purple, but another 5% of purple. So the mix is 10% purple instead of 5%.

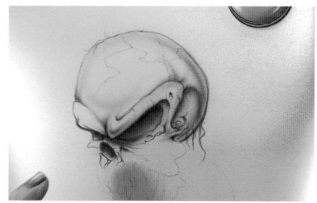

"Like the graphic, I start with a lighter tone, then use progressively darker tones as I build shadow areas. If you go too dark too quickly you have no color dynamics. The cooler the colors, the farther back they appear in any piece."

15

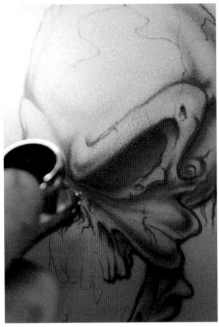

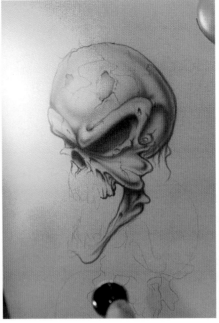

"You have to think about line dynamics. The lines on the bottom are heavier than on the top which...

...gives illusion of a heavier bottom side, that's the shadow side. Not to be used in portraiture. In more crazy styles I always do this."

Each part of the skull is created by a series of lines, some very, very fine. Eventually however, a detail like a tooth emerges.

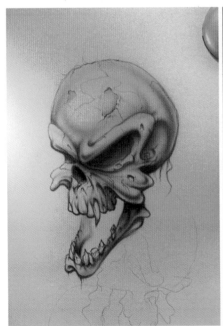

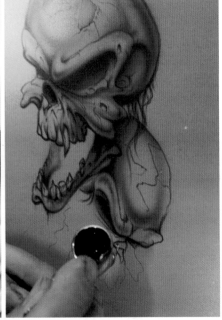

Progress shot shows one nearly completed skull. "I like my skulls to have lots of character and stay away from the text book medical school look."

"It's nice to use different methods, part of this is free hand, part of it I use a stencil to get a really clean line. It makes a more dynamic piece of art that way."

Now the second skull, a little smaller and a little more angular, emerges from behind the first,

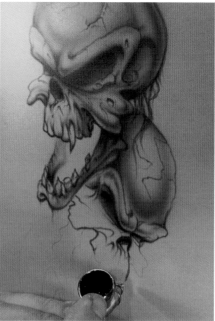

"Don't fight with the gun. If you think it's dirty stop and clean off the tip, I use a small sable brush and solvent to clean the gun tip."

With a clean airbrush Vince continues to develop the second skull. "They could be brothers but not identical twins."

Some areas require a nice clean line and for this Vince uses the stencil again.

handy. I test the mixture: by running a long continuous test line, the gun shouldn't spit as I do the line. And you should be able to get a nice gradient without any coarseness. As I do these skulls, I'm not thinking of lines that define the skull but rather the bottom of a shadow."

"When you're doing your lines, approach them with confidence. That way all the strokes combine to create the look you're after. If you're confident then the lines are smoother. You have to think about your light and dark areas, you can use these areas to push the surface off the canvas. When you put the areas near each other it gives the drawing a little tension. And be sure to hide any of the pencil lines you made earlier. I don't like to go into a mural with preconceived ideas of what it's going to look like. It's much better if it's spontaneous. Once again, I use a stencil to speed things up and create a dark area. A good piece of art should have sharp points, whether it's a tattoo or a piece of airbrush art."

Each skull is created with a series of lines, some so small they can barely be seen, made by holding the airbrush very close to the tank. Sometimes a series of lines seem almost random, until a tooth emerges from the apparent chaos, complete with highlights on the highest surface and a shadow on the lowest.

Vince explains that, "as the skulls get smaller you have to settle for less detail or all the lines just make it too dark. The major light and dark areas are the most important thing."

At this point the skulls are done. Vince uses a new mix of paint with more purple to darken the sockets and deepest shadows. Vince points out the fact that he is not using black to darken the shadows. Instead he adds the complimentary color to the mix to make a mock-black, "just jump to the other side of the color wheel and add that, it gets muddy but it isn't black. I'm always careful to test it on the palette first. That is, I spray it over the same color that's on the tank, not over white. The end result is subtle but readily noticeable."

The next step is white. As Vince explains, "I use it to tie the skulls together, it will be a vapor trail."

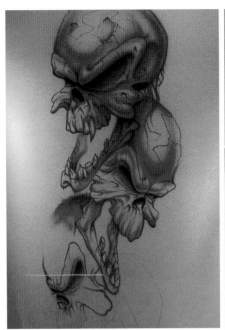

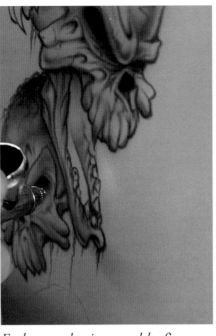

"You have to be sure to cover each of the pencil lines with paint so they disappear."

Each eye socket is created by first drawing in a heavy brow line, then filling the socket with progressively lighter shades that define it as a void.

Even the small skulls are rendered with care, one shadow at a time. "These are made with the same shadows, the same strokes, just on a smaller scale."

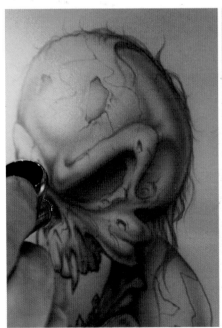

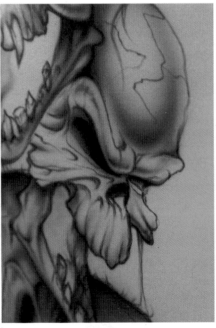

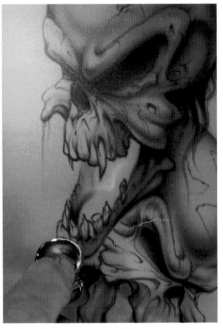

"On the small ones the mix is really important. You're moving so much air and so little paint. Down near the bottom I go to the slow reducer with one drop of retarder. And reduce the pressure to 30 psi."

"The eye sockets are darkened with dark purple (purple is compliment to orange) By adding its compliment you reduce the chroma of the original color making it less vibrant and thus darker appearing."

The white vapor trail is next, used to create the "other worldly feel"…

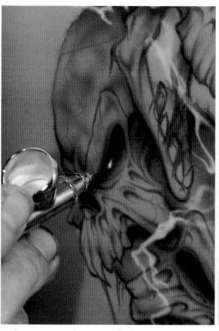

... and to tie all the skulls together. "Use eye candy sparingly, don't over do it, use it to create continuity."

The same white and the same small, detail, airbrush is used to create the evil gleam in the eyes.

Each set of eyes is slightly different from the others.

For this final detail work, Vince uses the same small detail airbrush seen earlier. The white is regular basecoat white. "Whichever system you're into. You have to be sure to cross over areas that are dark," explains Vince, "otherwise no one would see it. The white is also used to create the evil glimmer in the eyes. When I'm doing this I try to give each skull a slightly different eye."

"Now I shoot straight purple, just a very small amount mostly on top of the white. I try to keep the purple out of the yellow areas. And you have to know when to stop or you ruin the effect you're trying to create."

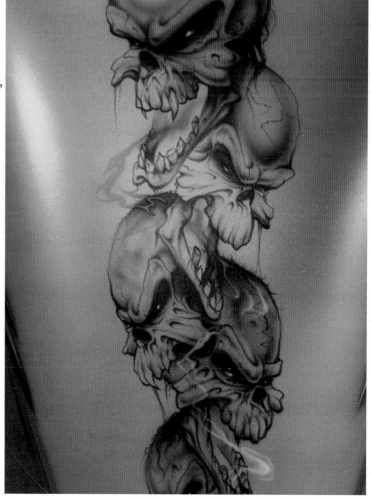

The finished mural.....One weird but happy family.

Q&A: Vince Goodeve

Vince, let's start with a little background on you and how you became an airbrush artist.

I've been around body shops since I was a kid, and if you hang around long enough they put you to work. By the time I was 10 years old I was wiping off cars with thinner and doing shop-rat stuff. My family is artistic, we have it in the blood. I would always draw with my dad and play games based on drawing. After high school I went to Ontario Collage of Art, for a month, but didn't like it. After OCA I worked at all kinds of part time jobs, but I kept working at my art. I invested in it all the time, and people would always buy what I did. I took some short classes or seminars. In one of those classes I met Morty, from Yonkers. He gave me real encouragement and offered to do private lessons. In a week I learned more than I learned in all the years before that.

How did you make the transition to full time airbrushing and art?

Back in the 1980s I went to the body shop and painted cars. The money was good, I did that for a couple of years. Then I needed to paint art, I was painting bikes on the side for three hundred dollars and I did T shirts and almost anything. Gradually, I was able to command better money for my paint jobs. I was associated with Bob McKay for a few years and he introduced me to a lot of good people. Then, when I won the VQ Best Painter award in 2001, that was a turning point, people really took notice at that point.

You always talk about color theory, can you expand on that a little?

I like color combinations, it's important which color you put next to the other color. You have a theory behind you, but you have to decide if it looks good or not. It has to pop.

When you nail the combination right it almost vibrates, it's either harmonious and peaceful, or chaotic.

Can you give an example of how you use the wheel?

Say you have a dominant hue, to knock it back I reach across the color wheel and add the color opposite to darken it. I seldom use black, black doesn't occur in nature, there's always other colors reflected onto the black.

What kind of paint do you like?

Honestly, the paints I use are the ones that are most available, it's more a matter of how you use the paints. PPG and House of Kolor have super quality and great longevity, but I break all the rules and mix things together that I'm not supposed to. As long as you have a good base in the chemistry you're OK. They say you can't mix products from different companies, but I do. I don't use a lot of flip flop paints, I would rather have the paint itself and the design carry the day, instead of using tricks.

Tell us why you like toners, and a little about the paint system you're bringing out?

Toners are the mixing system used to create certain colors, the PPG Global line is a good example. My goal is to come up with a color palette for people that is similar to what's available to artists. A lot of colors in the auto world are harsh, so I want to make available colors that are more like fine art. I want to make it possible for people to buy small quantities of these toners already mixed, grouped by convenience. The object is to make a color wheel, or chart, so people can buy a particular color, already mixed for airbrush use, and available in small quantities. We will work with Bear Air and should have our paint kits available in the future

Q&A: Vince Goodeve

What type or brand of airbrush do you prefer and why?

I've used Iwata since I picked up my first airbrush. They are well made, last a long time, and they fit my hand well. I especially like the performance of the Micron for really fine detail work.

Where do you get your ideas?

My mind has always been creative, I think about the structure and what I want to achieve, but really, it just happens. You can over-design a piece though. If too much energy goes in at the design phase then you have nothing left for the performance, it's like music. Sometimes when I work late at night, hours go by and it seems like minutes, and at the end I wonder, "who painted that piece."

How much do you use the computer?

Two years ago I didn't use it at all. But with help from friends, and some patience, I use it now to cut out all the linear stuff. You can only use it on things that are mildly curved, but the design phase is the same.

I tell people, "don't get married to one system, there's no one right way." Sometimes I use spray mask, sometimes I cut out by hand, it depends on the situation.

Any final words of advice?

Be careful, there's a point where you can be very big, but the danger is you loose the integrity of your artwork. I do everything from the bodywork to the basecoat and clearcoat because I want complete control. I don't like to farm out any of the work.

Vince working on "Time Warp," one of his favorite projects. "The bike covers 100 years of American History, 1900 to 2000."

"Rick Fairless (Strokers of Dallas) sent me images and ideas, but I had to decide which images to use and how big they should be."

Chapter Two

Steve Wizard

Reality Flames Surround a Chrome Eagle

Like most of the airbrushing sequences in this book, the creation of the chrome tribal-style eagle is really a two-part affair. First comes the eagle, then the flames. Steve Chaszeyka (aka The Wizard), from New Middletown, Ohio, starts with a drawing of the eagle and a piece of chalk. The paint work is being done on a new motorcycle for Logic Motorcycles in nearby Youngstown, Ohio. The Eagle originated "in my head" explains Steve.

Next he applies premask masking material,

The finished design, done for Logic Motorcycles, is a nice combination of two designs: a chrome eagle laid out over a set of reality-flames.

designed to transfer vinyl letters to a surface, to both sides of the tank. "I like the transparency of it," explains Steve, "it allows you to examine the look of your work, what you're exposing and what you're hiding." (The tank has already been painted with urethane base coat, clearcoated, and sanded with 600 grit paper.)

Before taping the drawing over the premask material, Steve coats the back of the drawing with chalk. Now the sketch is taped over the tank so Steve can run a pencil over the design. As he presses on the pencil, the outline of the design is transferred to the premask material. A light chalk line is left on the premask.

"You have to have the right amount of pressure on the Xacto knife as you do the cutout," explains Steve. "Too much and you cut into the basecoat or you cause the clearcoat to lift, then you are back to the drawing board. Cutting in the corners is kind of like driving a Masserati, you have to let off in the corners or you miss the turn and have to go back." A non-transparent material is used for masking off the rest of the tank so that what's left is just the shape of the eagle.

A duplicate sketch for the right side of the tank is traced out on the light table after placing the first sketch "upside down" on the light table.

Steve warns that, "when you tape the designs onto the tank you have to make sure they're positioned exactly the same on both sides of the tank."

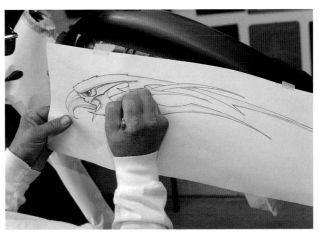

1) After attaching the premask to the tank, Steve lays the original sketch over the top, then traces the outline of the eagle with a pencil.

2) Because of the chalk on the backside of the sketch, the design is transferred to the premask material.

4) All the cut out pieces are carefully saved for use later in the project.

3) Cutting out the premask is very time consuming, as Steve says, "once you start to paint it goes pretty fast, but this part takes time."

The actual painting begins with pastel blue. These are the areas that will be highlights in the finished artwork.

Gradually, the beginnings of the design emerge from a series of highlights.

For many of these highlights, Steve starts with a small dot of paint...

At this point it's easy to make the out the stylized eagle.

...and then moves the airbrush rapidly across the tank from the dot toward the rear.

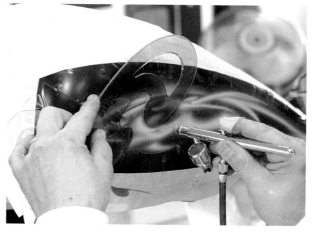

Masks or stencils are often used to contain the effects of one color (blue reflected from the sky in this case) to a small area.

APPLYING COLOR

The first color to go on is a pastel blue that looks almost white, "I'm putting this paint on in places where I imagine the highlights to be," explains Steve. The effect looks almost like a speed line on an illustration. Next, Steve mixes a darker blue. The idea is to duplicate the look of chrome by mimicking the mirror images that occur in chrome. "Chrome is only the reflection of things around it," explains Steve, "often blue from the sky with brown or green on the bottom depending on what the object is parked on. At the top I darken the chrome, because as a chrome object rolls around, at the top where it doesn't get as much light, it gets darker. That's the effect I'm trying to create. I'm a little ahead of myself but I want to go in here and make some highlights with pure white."

LOWER REFLECTIONS

Now Steve uses a "more reflective color on the bottom," dark grey and orange in this case, with a bit of brownish green. These colors are reflecting the ground that the object is sitting on. Close to the horizon line Steve adds black to the brownish-orange mix. "If you look at the reflection on a piece of chrome there is a horizon line and it's typically black, or nearly black." Steve will come back later and add more highlights to the "raised" parts of the

Continued on page 28

The lower edge of a chrome object reflects whatever it's sitting on - the ground in this case.

At this point you can clearly see the eagle's head and feathers done in light highlights and reflected blue.

Now, Steve adds pure white highlights.

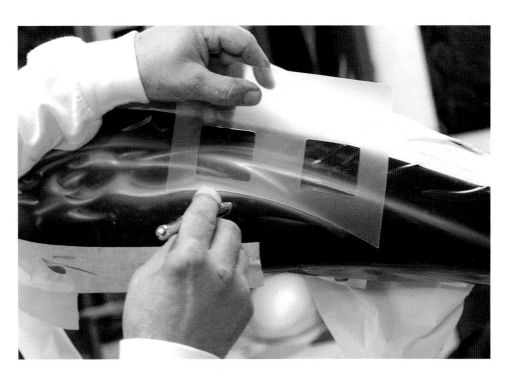

Masking tape is used to contain the effects of the "ground" colors to specific areas.

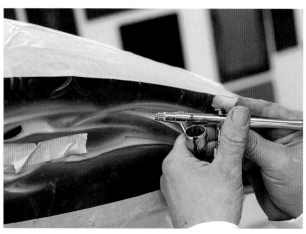

...a horizon line that flows along the chrome spear.

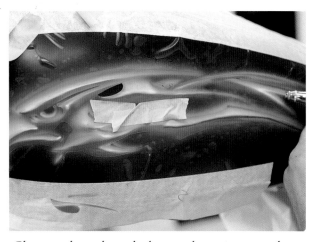

Close up shows how darker earth tones are used to create the horizon line.

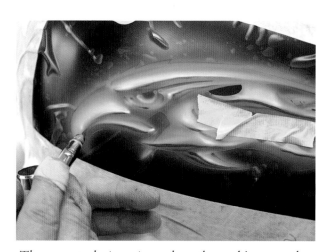

The same technique is used on the eagle's top and bottom beak.

A two-handed grip and careful trigger pull make for a clean, smooth line...

After creating the horizon line, Steve goes back later to darken it, by adding a small amount of black to the mix.

Q&A: The Wizard

Steve, give us a little background on you and how you became an airbrush artist?

I always had a knack for art, it always came naturally. There was this fella here in town, Guy Shively, he was my mentor. After seeing him I charged ahead and started pinstriping cabinets at home, the TV, cars in the garage. Over the years I developed a style. Airbrushing was my second pursuit. I thought I could make a dollar at that too. I'm self taught. At that time no one would teach you anything. Back then the big name was Greg of Akron, he inspired a lot of airbrushers, including me.

I did it part-time for years while I sold insurance or real estate. Then I went to work for a guy with a catalog company as an illustrator. And that was good. I learned I was good enough that this person would pay me, I had skills to contribute. In the meantime I'm going to car shows and making a thousand or two on a weekend. So I quit the catalog company and went out on my own. And it's been very fun and profitable since then. I've been on my own for twenty years.

What kind of paints do you like?

For striping it's One-Shot. I'm loyal to Mack brushes, they have a real feel for the artist. They are developing a brush with my name on it. A scroll brush. It suits my needs and style of striping. Other people think the magic is in the brush, it helps, but that's not all of it.

For airbrushing I like Spies Hecker paint, it's high pigmentation, light-fast with a lifetime guarantee. But nearly any basecoat system will work. House of Kolor has a great system too when you want unique colors. H of K has the tints you need for the reality flames.

Where do you get your ideas?

I have a lot of things in my head that are creative, like that eagle. Sometimes that flow is restricted 'cause the customer has an idea. He may want a wolf posed a certain way. I call that doing the dance, you have to reproduce the picture he gives you. The creativity is gone and it's mechanical at that point, but that doesn't make it any easier. And I have to give credit where credit is due. I'm really grateful to Mike Lavallee for sharing the formula for the reality flames.

When do you use a test panel?

I use them when there's a high risk the customer and I aren't on the same page as to how much the underlying marblizing or ghost-flames should show through. So I suggest he spend two hundred bucks and do "knock downs." These are three-part panels with the effect done three ways. Then the customer picks the one

he likes. And if he or she doesn't like any of them, maybe it's not someone I should work for.

To what do you attribute your success?

I attribute to my success to my wife and partner Carol. She's the driving force behind Wizard Graphics, and she keeps me "level." It also takes a lot of hard work. If you're waiting for that big break it ain't ever going to come. Back to the creative part, ideas that are new and fresh are hard to come by. A really successful artist like Chris Cruz can compose something unique and still his style and people love it, that's his strength.

You said earlier that this is a two-step process?

On a piece like this, the eagle and flames, you do them one at a time. Some guys do the flames, apply clear and then the eagle right on top, but I like working on black. Step one, work on the eagle, no distraction from the other art. Then cover that up and do the flames right over it, just "do the flames." Then when you uncover it, it's like MAN, this is great. But you do have to have the whole thing in your head when you start. You have to make sure the overall composition works together and fits the piece.

How much do you use the computer?

I use it when I have to cut lettering. And if something has to be repeated, like a logo. It's a wonderful tool for when you need an exact shape, it also saves you razor-blading into a paint job, the computer generated mask saves all that.

You said something about the art of observation?

When you look at the reference, when you're trying to match feathers or chrome or whatever, you need to know when to use the airbrush or hand-brush.

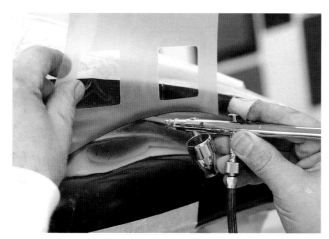

Steve keeps a number of masks and stencils handy for precision work.

Pieces of premask, cut out earlier, were saved on the window...

...and can be used now.

horizon line, so it looks natural (usually the part of the chrome piece closest to the camera or eye will be a highlight or star of sunlight).

Small masks are used throughout the process (note the photos) to contain the effect of a color to one small area. Most of this job is done with what Steve calls a "middle of the road Iwata airbrush."

THE BEVELED EDGES

Pieces of the design that were cut out earlier are now used again as masks. The part of the mask that is laid down is then trimmed at the very edge, because this "new edge" will end up being a reflective surface (note the photos on the next page).

After pulling the edge of the masks off the areas that will be beveled, Steve sprays the area with white, with a few highlights. Light orange is used to create a gold-colored edge on the bottom of the bevel, this will be the reflection of the flames that will be added later.

A RIVETING TOPIC

Steve thinks a few rivets might be a good addition to the eagle, explaining, "They detract from the smoothness of the piece, but they add good mechanical detail." Just to be sure they're going to work Steve tries them on the test panel before putting them on the tank.

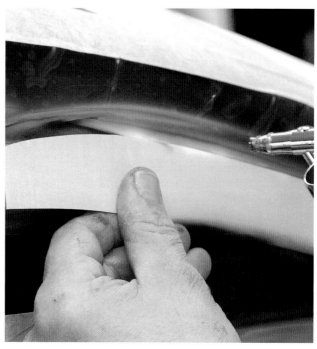

Using white paint and a stencil, Steve begins creating highlights on the uppermost area of the chrome.

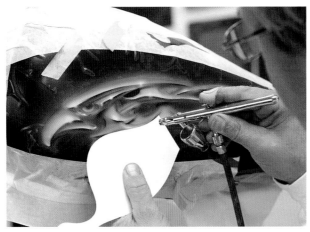

Here Steve uses another stencil as he creates one more highlight on the very edge of the chrome.

At this point part of the mask, cut out earlier, is put back down and the Xacto knife...

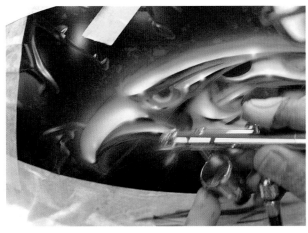

More highlights on the beak, done freehand this time.

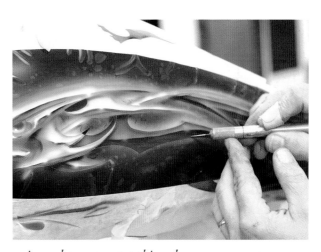

...is used to cut out a thin edge.

A progress picture, note how the highlights help to raise the chrome off the tank and enhance the 3-D effect.

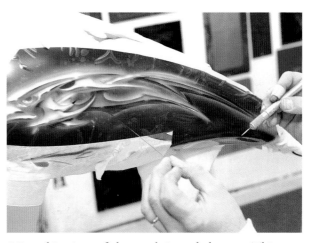

Now this piece of the mask is peeled away. This area will be the beveled edge.

Now the upper part of the mask is trimmed to create another beveled edge.

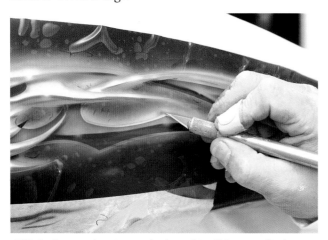

With the mask trimmed, the white/blue applied earlier shows through.

Happy with the test results, Steve puts the mask on the eagle. The first color is white, "we are doing the highlights first partly because that's the paint that's in the gun." Just because these rivets are small doesn't mean they aren't a lot of work. Next, he puts the dots back on the design and creates the highlights on the bottom of each rivet.

"When I want detail like this I turn the air pressure down to 10 or 15 pounds," explains Steve, "normally it's 35 or 40 psi. The gun I'm using is an Iwata revolution." Finishing the rivets requires that Steve mask and unmask the area a number of times so he can create the level of detail necessary to make these look like convincing rivets. The actual sequence of events is best explained by the photos and captions.

REALITY FLAMES

Before starting in on the flames Steve masks off the eagle with Transfer Rite Ultra made by American Biltrite Inc. As Steve explains, "I'm covering over the eagle (some call it back masking) so I can spray the flames without any over-spray on the eagle.

The process of creating the reality flames might seem intimidating. In fact, Steve recalls being, "terrified when I first saw these flames." Like most complex tasks, this one becomes less intimidating when it's broken down into a series of steps. In this case, there are ten steps to the reality flames.

Now highlights can be added to the just-exposed beveled edges. Note: The eagle and most of the pre-flame work is done with Spies Hecker paints.

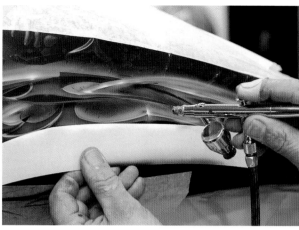

You can see how white paint and a stencil have been used to create a star at the intersection of two beveled edges.

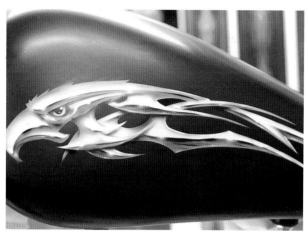

Progress photo of a chrome, tribal-eagle complete with horizon line and beveled edges.

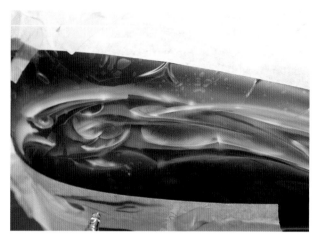

A progress shot. Note how the lower beveled edges reflect the red of the flames - which haven't been created yet.

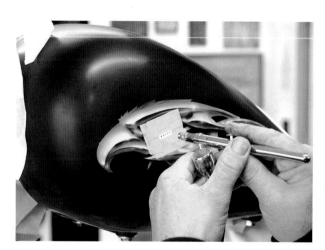

Steve decided to add detail, in the form of a set of rivets on the side of the eagle.

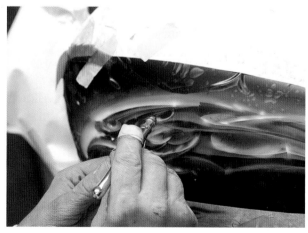

Before finishing this part of the project Steve adds a few more white highlights.

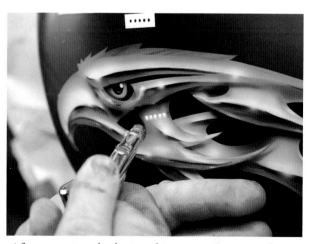

After spraying the basic white rivet, Steve masks each rivet and adds a highlight on the bottom.

31

1) *Before taking the masks off the rivet heads Steve adds shadows around each rivet to help "sink" it into the metal.*

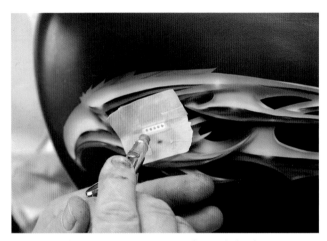

2) *Now the masks are "swapped" and shadows are added to the lower edge of each rivet.*

3) *Next a bright highlight is added to each rivet with a drop of white paint.*

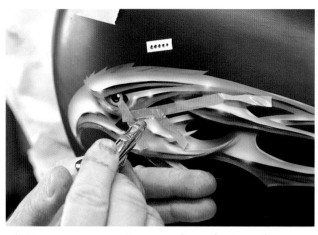

4) *To create a seam Steve masks each rivet, then runs masking tape along the edge of the seam followed by a little dark paint.*

Step 1: House of Kolor moly orange (SG 103 Q01) is the first color you put down. Steve calls this, "the foundation for all the rest, this will be the background for the flames." As the photos show, Steve puts this moly orange down freehand without the use of any masking or stencils.

Step 2: Steve calls this, "knocking it back" with candy apple red. "This makes the orange mysterious, enhances the highlights and darkens the shadows." The paint is kandy koncentrate (KK 11) from H of K mixed 3 to 1 (one part KK 11) with SG 100, an intercoat clear. "I put this on fairly heavy with a conventional touch up gun (a Sata mini jet HVLP), running at 35 psi."

Step 3: More moly orange. "I'm using a template to reinforce some of the shapes we did earlier," explains Steve. "And also adding new shapes."

Step 4: Candy tangerine (KK 08) applied over the moly orange.

Step 5: Chrome yellow (SG 102) reduced 25 to 50 % and applied with a template. Suddenly the reds are redder - partly by contrast with the yellow nearby. Steve warns that, "when you get near the end of the project it's easy to just rush through the last parts of the job. There's a lot of standing back and looking at a job like this, comparing one side of the tank to the other, or the front fender to the rear, to make sure the job is consistent."

Continued on page 37

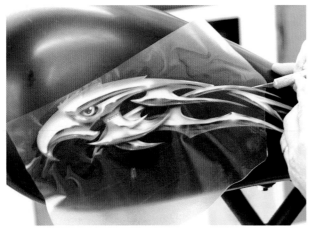

Time for reality flames, but first a little masking with clear material.

...in a pattern...

The first color is moly orange.

...that suggests the licks of a campfire.

These early licks are applied freehand...

Steve keeps at it until the entire side of the tank is engulfed in random red licks.

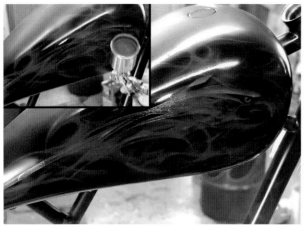

The candy apple red is next, applied over the moly orange, followed by a coat of intercoat clear.

A progress shot at the end of the moly-orange-with-stencil step number 3.

More moly orange follows, but applied this time with a stencil.

A mist of candy tangerine (step number 4) has been misted over the moly orange to richen the colors.

Note how the use of the stencil gives definition to the flames.

The chrome yellow (step number 5) is applied with a stencil to brighten the flames.

Still working on step 5, chrome yellow (with extra reduction) sprayed on with a stencil.

A progress shot, after the candy tangerine. The effect is to mute the yellow and enhance the reds.

A progress shot at the end of the chrome-yellow phase.

Step number 7, the addition of more chrome yellow.

Step 6, a mist of candy tangerine over the whole thing, done with a small touch-up gun.

By doing the flames in layers the whole thing takes on the semi-transparent look of a real fire.

Another progress shot at the end of step number 7.

Step 9, a few white highlights on the edges of the flames.

Step 8 is the addition of candy yellow...

After step 10, a light mist of pagan gold.

...which brightens the chrome yellow already applied.

Now Steve can pull the mask to see the full effects of this multi-step project.

Each step, each layer, takes time. The template gives the flames edges. "If you don't use the template the flames have a soft, out-of-focus look."

Step 6: Steve applies a mist of candy tangerine (KK 08) on everything.

Step 7: More chrome yellow basecoat, reinforcing the heat of the fire, "You have to constantly cut new stencils,"says Steve. "Because they get a paint buildup at the edge and if you aren't careful it will transfer to the tank. Yellow reality flames only look good on orange, if you make a new flame shape on the black, with yellow, it doesn't look right."

Step 8: Kandy yellow. (KK 02). "Some painters use pagan gold. This will brighten the yellow."

Step 9:White basecoat (BC 26 White Q 01), applied sparingly with a stencil to create small highlights on the yellow edges and points.

Step 10: Steve mists on a little bit of pagan gold.

Now it's time to pull the mask. The only thing left is a few highlights (shown on this page) done with white paint and a "slotted template." Steve explains that there is one more step (one that isn't shown). "You can take black or your base color, and emphasize the hollows, but you have to be real selective as you do this."

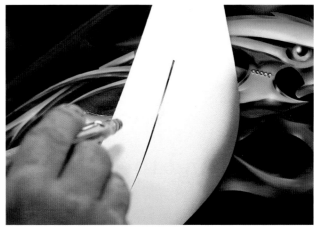

What Steve calls a "gleam" or highlight is done with this homemade stencil.

The effect enhances the feel of chrome, but needs to be used with discretion.

The finished machine. Though we only covered the tank, Steve painted both fenders, the oil tank and even the frame's neck.

Chapter Three

John Nicholas of K.C. Creations

Beauty and the Beast

The airbrush creation seen here is as complex as any in the book. Designed and painted by John Nicholas at KC Creations in Overland Park, Kansas, the painting combines a pinup with a skull, a set of reality flames, a poker hand and an extremely detailed bottle of Whiskey. The starting point is the basecoat of platinum metallic (MBC02, Q01) from House of Kolor, with a clearcoat.

John starts by wet sanding the clearcoat with

Known as "Man's Ruin," the graphic painted on the tank of this custom bike is actually the melding of five separate images.

800 grit to knock down the shine. Everything is sanded except the seams and high points. Those areas are scuffed with grey scotchbrite because, as John explains, "you don't want to sand those areas with sand paper because you might sand through.'

To create the main image, John uses transfer paper (Frisket film) to trace an image from a calendar. The transfer paper has a sticky back. John sticks it down onto the tank and works out the bubbles before masking off the rest of the tank. John extends the drawing slightly making the legs longer, explaining as he does, "this is the area where the image will fade out."

The image is cut out now, and pulled off the tank so the actual painting can begin. The first coat of paint is black, "this is so we don't have the metallic effect," explains John, "and it also means we won't show a white line at the very edge when we pull the masking paper. To mix the skin tone paint I use white, red, yellow, and a little green. You can add a little black if you want to tone it down but you don't want to make it muddy. You can also use transparent red oxide (Deltron DMD 623) over white as a skin tone, but you have to add a layer of intercoat clear before adding any highlights or the highlights will blend right into the skin tone and make them brown."

John often uses an existing photograph or illustration as the start of his airbrush design.

Working on a light table, John does a detailed tracing onto Frisket paper.

After peeling the Frisket from the picture, John sticks it onto the tank and works out the bubbles with a squeegee.

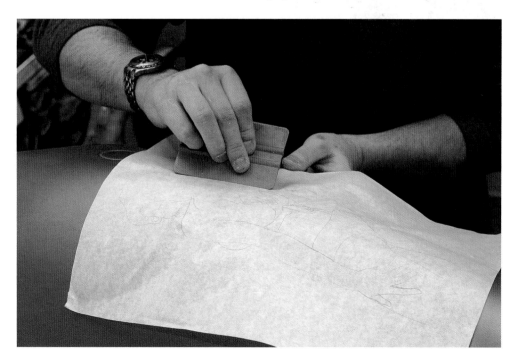

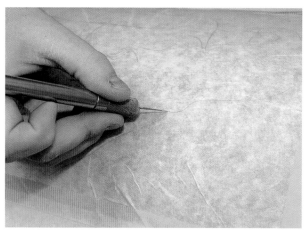

"Cutting out is like pinstriping with a knife, the knife needs to be sharp as the devil or you don't cut all the way through."

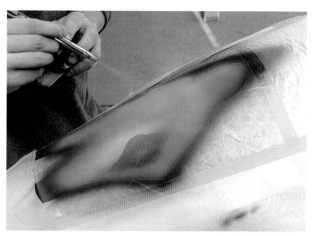

The special-mix skin tone paint is applied to the area uniformly. "Keep in mind you want to start where you imagine the highlights to be."

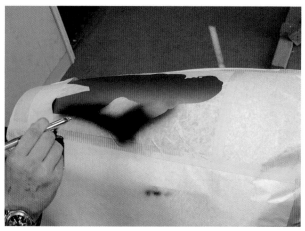

The first coat of paint is basecoat black, applied with one of John's Iwata Eclipse HP-BCS airbrushes.

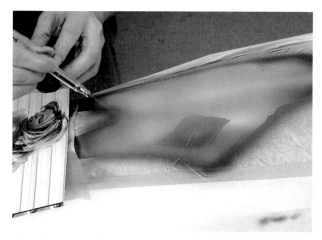

"I often work from dark to light, and then from light to dark."

Here you can see the finished basecoat, now the real painting can begin.

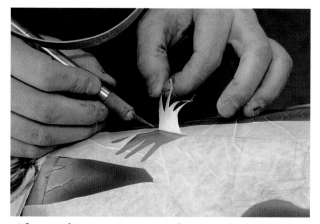

After applying an intercoat clearcoat (DBC 500) and allowing it to dry, John puts the stencil back onto the tank, then pulls back selected areas he wants to paint.

"I always put any new color in a bottle that had a similar color in it last, so any residue left in the bottle won't hurt the new color. In this case I put the skin tone mixture in a bottle that had red in it. I don't want to put this color in a bottle that had metallic in it because even a little fleck of metallic will kill my skin tones. I've mixed the paint with PPG 870, medium-speed reducer".

HIGHLIGHTS

Now come the highlights and details, "It's all the same color at this point," says John. "I don't want to kill it all at once. I'm going to put on a heavy coat of intercoat clear because if I put frisket film back on it will pull the paint, but the clear will lock it down." During the work John works hard to minimize film thickness, "I don't like to use the big gun because it puts out so much paint and creates an edge you have to deal with later."

Next the stencil is put back down and various parts are pulled up so John can do detail painting on those areas with more flesh tone mix.

Heavier applications of flesh tone paint are used to create highlights that define the image. Gradually a hand and arm arise from the cut out area. Eventually, John sticks the arm back down and pulls the next area. "Sometimes the stencil gets so beat up that you have to hold it in place with extra tape," explains John, "or just make a new piece. This is all a matter of light and dark, I'm always going from one to the other."

"Now I'm going to mix up a special color for toning. I want black, but I want it to be transparent. I mix black and transparent red oxide, reduced a lot so it has a transparent quality. Transparent red oxide (aka trans-red-oxide) is sort of a dye so I have to be careful how much of it I use. PPG and House of Kolor use the same reducer. I use both systems. Sometimes I use Dupont, but then I have to use their reducer."

SHADOWING

John explains how he uses the new paint, "First I bring the light up, then I put shadows in with the over-reduced black color I just mixed."

Continued on page 44

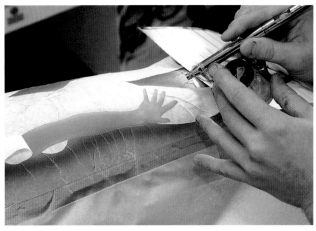

Heavier applications of the skin-tone paint are used to create highlights on the hand and arm.

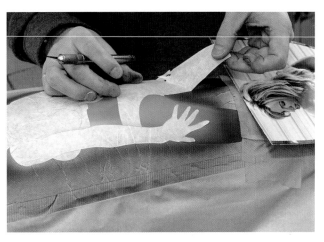

After working on the arm, John puts that part of the stencil back down and pulls the paper off the legs.

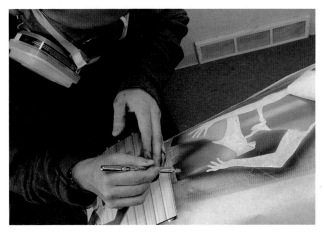

Again, heavier applications of the same skin-tone paint are used to create highlights like the one on the side of her leg.

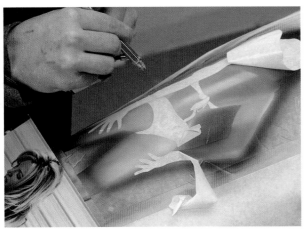

"Some pieces are pulled for shadow lines and some for highlights, I do the highlights freehand first."

More shadows define the line where the fingers meet the legs.

After mixing the "toning" color John starts to create shadows, explaining as he does, "First you have to know where your light source is."

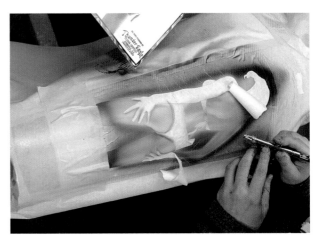

Careful application of the nearly transparent toning paint creates a very life-like shadow on the back of her right arm.

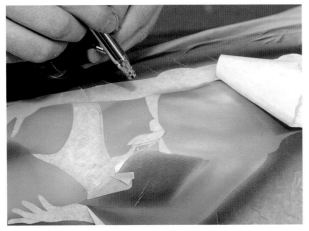

More of the same darker tone is used to create shadows on the pinup's back. "The black is thinned way down with DT 870, but don't get it too thin."

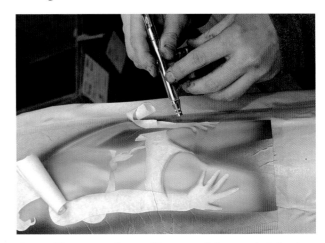

By pulling up only small areas of the mask John is able to keep a particular effect confined to one precise area.

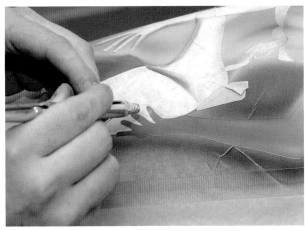

More skin-tone paint is used to create highlights on each individual finger.

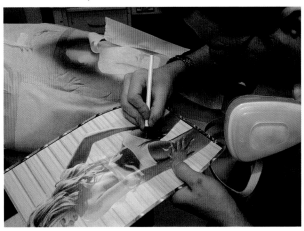

For detail areas John makes another mask from clear material.

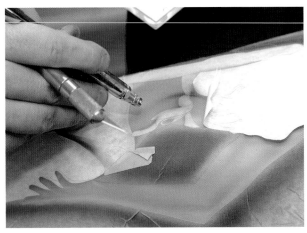

The image evolves slowly, much of it a matter of highlight and shadow, like that being sprayed onto her back.

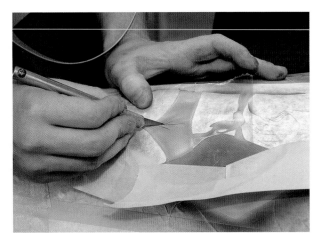

Now the mask is transferred to the painting, then cut and pulled back wherever John needs a shadow…

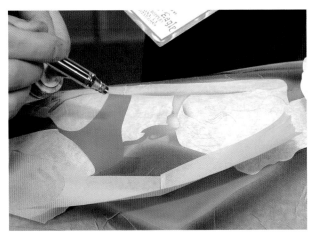

Masks are put in place around the swimsuit. Like the body areas, the swimsuit will be defined by highlights and shadows.

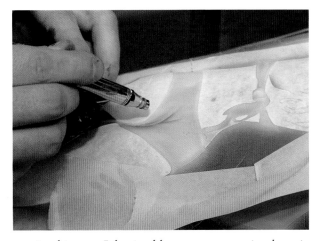

… in this way John is able to put creases in the suit that perfectly match the photograph. For detail work like this John uses 15 instead of 20 psi.

43

While the DBC intercoat clear is still wet, John sprinkles House of Kolor flake material on to mimic the sequins in the photograph.

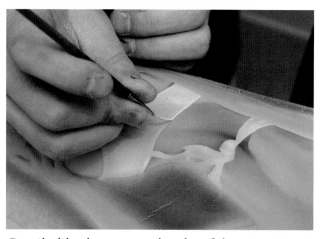

Details, like the seam on the edge of the swimsuit, are best created with a Painters Touch 2050 Script fine line multimedia brush using water-based paint.

Using transparent red oxide (see text), John tints all the skin tones in a few light passes. "This mixture needs to be on the thin side so it's not so grainy and you have more control. Thin with DT 870."

On the next page you can see how John creates shadows and darker areas on her back with the light semi-transparent toner. If one of the shadows goes too dark, John just comes back over it with a little of the original flesh tone color.

As was done before, John pulls various parts of the main mask so the effect he's after is contained to one small area. To paint the swim suit he puts the masks back down on either side of the suit. Working on the suit is, again, a matter of developing light and dark areas. To get the shadow details just right, John makes a second temporary mask from clear material, and then pulls part of this new mask out of the way to paint in the dark areas (see the preceding page).

John often uses water-based paints, applied with a brush, in conjunction with the airbrush work (the paint typically comes from COM.-Art or Createx). "But if you use water-based paint," explains John, "then you have to clear it with inter-coat clear before proceeding or the paint will be wiped off when they wipe the job down with wax and grease remover. Water-based is nice for that reason though, because you *can* wipe if off if you don't like the effect, without wiping off anything else."

Now, with many of the masks back in place, John tints all the skin tones with a light mist of transparent red oxide. And in the familiar pattern the highlights come next. These are done in white, though it doesn't stay bright white - the paint will darken a little as it blends and melts into the paint underneath. Some of the shadows are darkened with shading black for the dark shadows while others are darkened with transparent red oxide. At this point John does another coat of intercoat clear to lock it all down,

Time now to create another mask for the face and the hair. This is made from the same clear transfer material used earlier. The dark areas like eyelashes and eyebrows are cut out from the mask after it is placed on the tank (see the next page).

"For eyebrows I use hardly any paint, otherwise it turns into a dark brown line. Later I go in and dab on some water-based paint with a brush. When people do faces they put on too much paint, less is more. For lips they want to do red, I

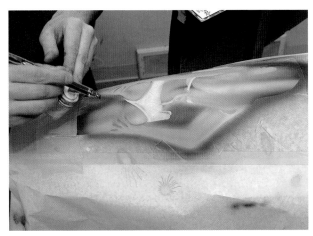

After warming up the skin tones, John works on highlights again, using basecoat white.

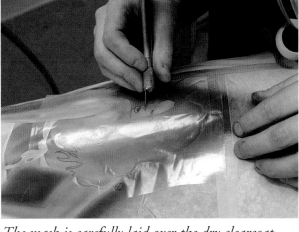

The mask is carefully laid over the dry clearcoat, then small areas like lips and eyelashes are slit and pulled back.

More transparent red oxide is used on specific shadows to tint them brown instead of black.

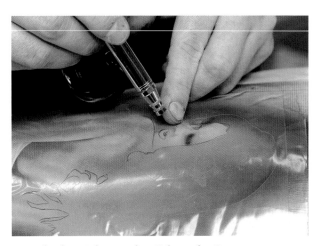

For the lips John applies "oh so thin" magenta paint.

Before airbrushing the facial details, John creates another mask on clear mask material. Before putting this down John will spray on another clearcoat.

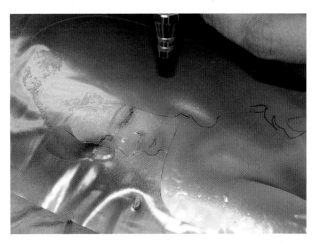

To get the right color on the lips, John applies the magenta in a number of light coats.

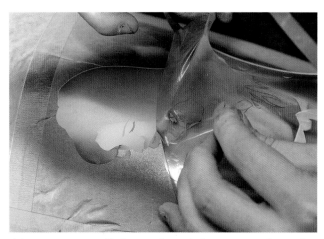

Time now to pull the mask and do some work on the facial details with a small brush.

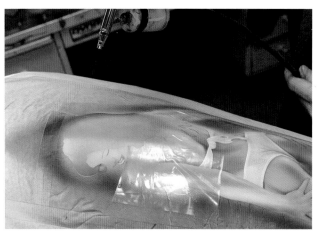

The foundation for the blonde hair is a coat of the same paint used for the skin tones.

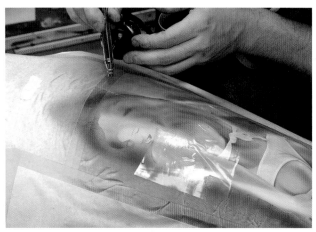

To create the shadows John uses shading black as shown, followed by just a little white. "I stress the word 'little' and the use of quick passes for the white."

use magenta. Magenta, thinned down, is like a pink. It goes on transparent and picks up skin tones underneath." After the multi-step creation on lips, John rolls back the mask and does the left shoulder.

HAIR AND FACIAL DETAILS

John starts with more flesh-color for foundation of the hair, explaining, "If you really look, the hair is about the same color as her skin." Then he starts adding shading black, at random. Next, he goes over it with a little white for highlights. The eyeliner is done with shading black. I haven't used any true black here," explains John, "because it's not a real color." Details are done with transparent black and white, water-based, by brush. And finally John does a clearcoat over the whole thing with the big gun.

SHIFTING GEARS

At this point John masks over the pinup and starts spraying straight black and candy black on the surrounding area, "this will be background, I will have it fade as it gets farther away from the figure." The paint however, is not lying down evenly on the tank, so John stops painting and starts cleaning with wax and grease remover, then water-based cleaner, adding, "the water-based will remove any static electricity.

Next he goes back and fades the black onto the bottom of her legs and sprays in a little transparent red oxide at edges of the body so the black blends better with the flesh tones.

JIM BEAM

The first step is to trace the Jim Beam image onto frisket transfer paper and apply that to the tank. Next John masks off the surrounding area and begins the job of cutting out the main label from the transfer paper. This is what John calls, "the most time consuming part of the job." He also masks over the mask remaining on the tank, so the lines in his sketch aren't covered by paint. The actual painting starts with black followed by two coats of basecoat white.

Now the mask of the main label is re-applied to the tank and the mask for the label on the neck is cut out, pulled off, and the area painted white over black.

Continued on page 50

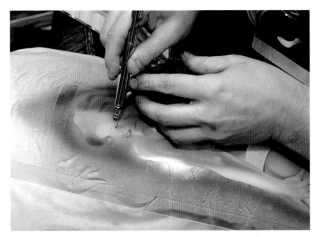

Holding the brush close, shading black is used to create eyeliner.

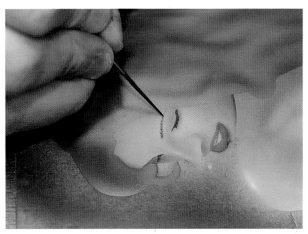

Water-based black and a steady hand are used to fill in the eyebrows…

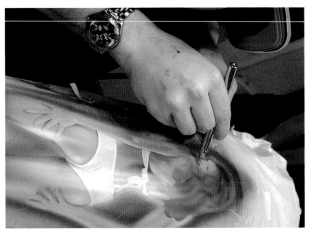

Details are created by holding the airbrush very close. "I use less air pressure, thinner paint and a few hand made stencils."

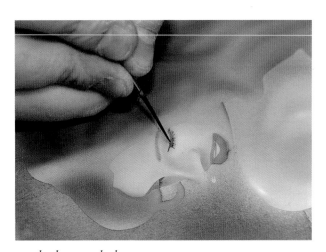

…the long eyelashes…

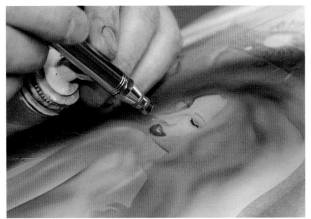

White is used to create highlights on the nose. "Get in close but make sure you spray a fat mist of paint through the airbrush off to the side first. This lessens the chance of spitting and having an 'oops.'"

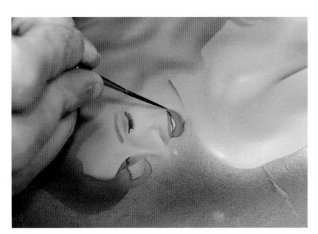

…and the fine details around her mouth.

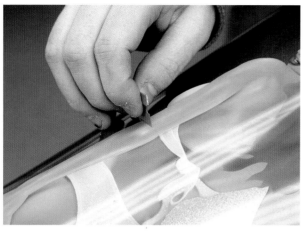

A razor blade is run carefully along any edges to minimize their thickness and make clearcoating easier.

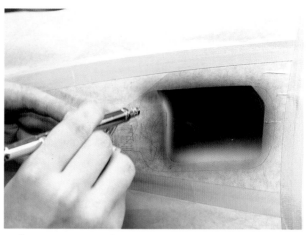

After cutting out the main label, John applies two coats of basecoat white.

After putting a clear mask over the pinup, John sprays black around the figure, allowing the black to fade toward the outer edges.

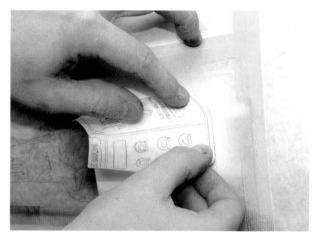

John puts the main label back on the Jim Beam bottle before cutting and removing another area of mask.

The next part of the image, the Jim Beam bottle, is traced onto a piece of Frisket paper before being applied to the tank.

The special color, bourbon-in-glass, starts as black with highlights in silver followed by a mist of trans-red-oxide and more white for highlights.

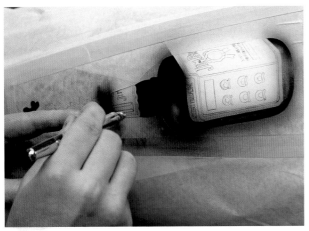

The final touch for the main part of the bottle is to make the highlights brighter with white basecoat applied to the brightest part of each highlight.

Then the mask for the center seal is replaced...

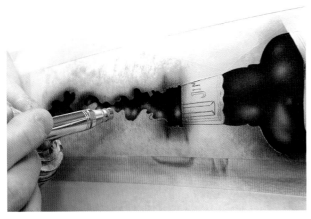

The spilled hooch is created in much the same way as the bottle, with the same basic set of colors and highlights in silver, (shown) with white used later.

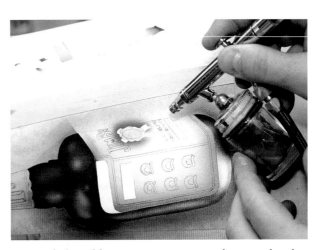

... and the ribbon area is cutout and painted red over white, making the red bright without too much buildup.

To duplicate the center part of the mask John cuts out the inner label and applies white followed by red.

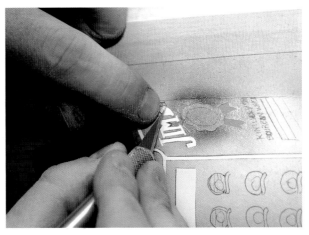

With a steady hand and a sharp knife, John cuts out the letters on the main label.

Now the letters and part of the side label are painted with solid black basecoat (DMD 683).

To duplicate the look of glass without any bourbon behind it, John cuts out that area and applies silver over the trans-red-oxide.

All the small letters and lines are done by hand, following lines left in the paint earlier by the knife.

With both label areas painted white and back-masked, John pulls the mask for the amber-colored bottle. The bottle area is painted black, highlights are added in silver, the whole area is toned with trans-red-oxide, then a little white is added to the highlights. The color of the spilled whiskey is created by spraying black around the edges (after pulling the masks), then going over that with two light applications of trans-red oxide, and eventually the highlights (later).

Creating a life-like label with all the necessary detail required many small cutouts, painting, back masking followed by a considerable amount of brush work. Much of this work it better explained by the photos on nearby pages.

"For much of this cutting out, I do want cut lines," explains John. "I want the Xacto knife to leave a line in the paint underneath, because I will use that as a guide when I come in later and do the pinstripes and letters by hand. In this situation, with water-based paint and such a fine line, the scriptwriter type brush is a better choice than a standard pinstriping brush."

"The other nice thing about this water-based paint is the fact that it dries flat, with very little film build up or edge. It makes the clearcoating easier later. When I get to a part where I feel like I might mess it up by going too far I lock it in with an application of clear."

At this point John starts on the deck of cards, a section we've left out due to space considerations and the fact it's the simplest part of this paint job.

After creating the deck of cards, John switches back to the Jim Beam bottle. First a mask is made from clear material, then slits are cut where John wants highlights in the neck. Now he sprays the area with silver. At the very end of the bottle John creates highlights on the threads, following the same procedure. While he's in the neighborhood John adds highlights to the spilled liquid.

At the bottom of the tank John applies clear masking material, then draws out more spilled liquid, then cuts it out. The idea is to have the spilled liquor at the bottom of the tank and have it catch fire with reality flames. "People say, 'why didn't you add those bubbles of the liquor when

A clever way to create highlights: first apply clear masking material and cut a series of slits that reach around the neck.

The third part of this montage, the skull, is formed freehand, starting with thinned down black basecoat.

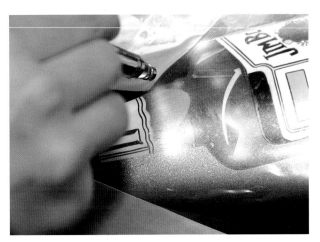

Then apply silver paint for highlights.

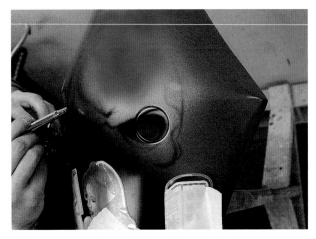

The eyes come first, followed by the beginning outlines of the skull.

Here you can see the finished area, complete with hand painted details and highlights in white and silver (note, a few small areas of the bottle were further detailed later).

Highlights in silver are added all through the project, rather than at the very end.

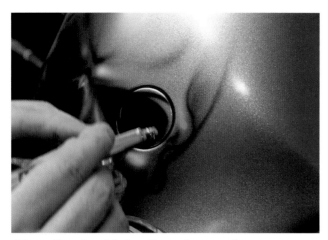

More silver is added to form the curved area just outside the eye socket.

The shape of the cheekbones is likewise formed with silver highlights.

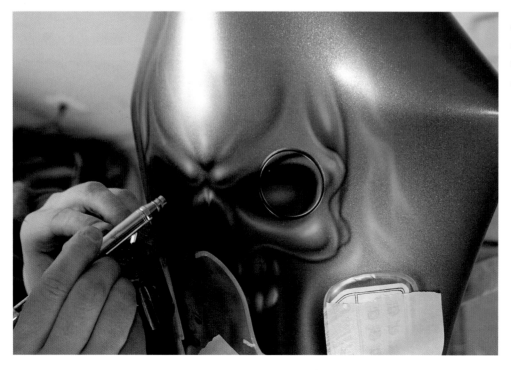

you did the bottle,?'" says John. "But at that time I didn't know how everything was going to fit together. It's easier to do it this way, the piece comes together better, and the masking isn't as complicated."

THE SKULL

I've done a lot of skulls," says John, "and I always do the eyes first. The first color is basecoat black thinned down. I start by going light to dark, then I go from dark to light." The job requires the use of basecoat black, candy black, silver for highlights and at the very end, blue pearl. This is another sequence where the photos do a better job of telling the story than the story does.

JOHN'S REALITY FLAMES

The formula for these reality flames is a little different than some others and actually starts with white.

The white is applied freehand to the edges of the spilled whiskey. John applies the paint with the tip close to the work, so it appears the wispy flames are coming off the top of the liquid. Medium chrome yellow, (DMD 639) thinned down, is the next color, applied on top of the white.

Basecoat orange is next. John keeps the tip close and free-hands the licks, one at a time. John decides to put a little more black on the bottom of

Now candy black is used to make a shadow just under some of the highlights.

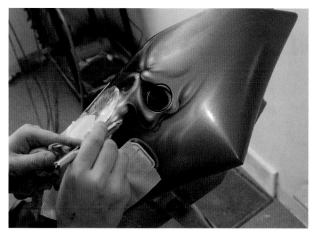

The same silver paint is used to form the evil teeth.

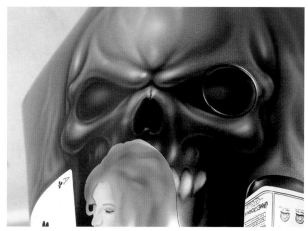

A quick look at the finished skull.

Highlights are developed further with the application of more silver to specific small areas.

The reality flames emerge from the spilled bourbon, as though someone put a match to the fire-water. John stars with white highlights on the spilled liquid.

The piece 'de résistance, an evil gleam from deep in the sockets, is done in blue pearl.

The next step is thinned-down, medium chrome yellow, applied on top of the white.

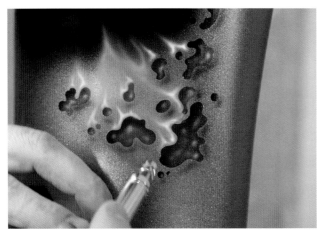

Each of the white wisps is topcoated with thinned down yellow (medium chrome yellow DMD 639) to form what will be the hottest part of the fire.

The next step is basecoat orange (or molly orange)...

...which John applies "freehand like a free-flowing ribbon, the way it flips and twists."

the tank, followed by more orange licks. "Flames are a lot like painting liquids," explains John, "but the shiny spots are reversed."

Candy red is applied next, over all the orange. Followed by more orange again to highlight hot spots and highlight the tips of the flames and the area where the fire is coming from, "those are the hottest spots."

The next color is yellow, applied in much the same way as the preceding coat of orange. The yellow adds heat and helps to define each flame lick.

A little candy orange makes it all brighter. "Then I go back in with white to create the white hot spots, where it originates." Now a little yellow, on top of the white. John finishes with a few silver details added to the base of the fire for shine in the blobs of whiskey.

Continued on page 57

"Candy red is applied to orange parts of fire only. Be careful at this point not to get any candy red on the skin tones or they will become pink and look very wrong."

"More candy apple red is applied over the orange - just enough to make the orange red. This gives more depth than straight red."

...close up shows how the yellow gives each lick more definition and makes them all much brighter.

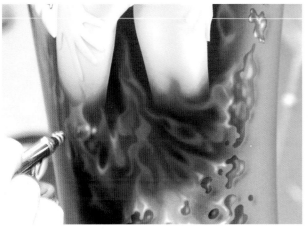

The red is followed by more orange, applied this time to just the tips.

A little white is used to make hot spots at the base of the fire...

A little yellow is added to the upper part of the licks...

...which is followed by the same yellow used earlier in the sequence.

John even uses a little silver in small precise areas to create just the right color.

"Once I have the texture right I use some black to blend everything together so it isn't too bright."

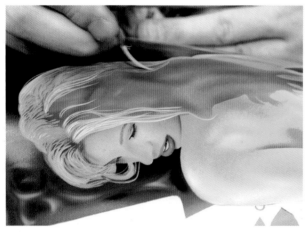

To create the realistic hair John mixes up white, yellow, red and a little green (the basic flesh-tone formula) with the water-based paints.

Next step - spray some yellow and TRO to make her blonde (not shown), followed by more brush work with yellow water-based, tinted with a little white.

The paint is applied by hand, "It all comes together one brush stroke at a time."

A little black is used again to create shadows. This is thinned down black mixed with a little trans-red-oxide.

Creating the hair with realistic texture is a matter of multiple details added over time.

The final step is to give the hair a rich sheen with a light mist of trans-red-oxide.

FINAL DETAILS

The only thing left are a few details on the hands and the hair. To make a flesh tone paint John mixes white, yellow, red, and a little green. Using a brush and the flesh-tone mix, John adds details like fingernails to the hands (not shown).

Using the same paint and another brush, John actually paints in the hair by hand. To blend it all together he adds a mist of black with the airbrush. Next, from the airbrush, comes the chrome yellow basecoat (diluted).

Using the airbrush, John does a mist of yellow and trans-red oxide (not shown) followed by more brush work using white mixed with a little yellow.

"I have to be careful that the color I use for the hair isn't too yellow." explains John. Occasionally John does a mist of black to tone it down and blend it together. The final coat of color is a mist of trans-red oxide which gives the hair just the right tone.

The finished piece. "But before putting everything away be sure to put a thin wet coat of intercoat clear on all the work so the water-based details won't be damaged during final wipe down."

Chapter Four

Lenni Schwartz

A Particularly Ghoulish Set of Skulls

Skulls are a bit like people, they come in every size and shape imaginable. The skulls seen here are the work of Lenni Schwartz of Krazy Kolors in Oakdale, Minnesota. Perhaps best known as the artist who does the art, graphics and flames for long-time bike builder Donnie Smith, Lenni is equally comfortable with pinstripe brush, or airbrush. The original idea here was to create two skulls, one holding the other, with the flames of hell licking up onto both.

Quality takes time. Creation of this grisly form took time, patience and a very specific set of steps.

No Computers

Lenni doesn't use a computer, so step one is to sketch out the art work in pencil, then trace that image onto a piece of Gerbermask. Transfer paper is then applied to the top of the Gerbermask, the backing removed and the whole thing is positioned on the tank as shown in the nearby photos.

After peeling off the transfer paper Lenni uses a squeegee to eliminate the inevitable bubbles, then physically slits the Gerbermask to eliminate stubborn bubbles.

The mask is cut into sections, according to the original sketch, before being applied to the tank. As Lenni explains, "I hate cutting on the tank, though sometimes you have to." Lenni can now pull the first section of the mask, which defines much of the face and part of the jaw for the upper skull. Highlights are now sprayed in this area using an Iwata airbrush and House of Kolor basecoat white (BC 26).

1) After doing the sketch and transferring that to Gerbermask, Lenni applies transfer paper over the top and then cuts out the image.

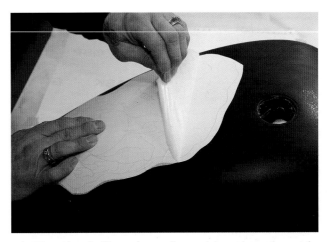

2) Now the skull mask can be positioned on the tank and the transfer paper peeled off.

4) And now the area that defines the upper skull can be pulled out.

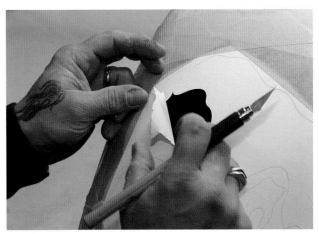

3) The mask was cut into sections before being applied to the tank...

Lenni starts the work with basecoat white, working to establish the brow and cheekbones...

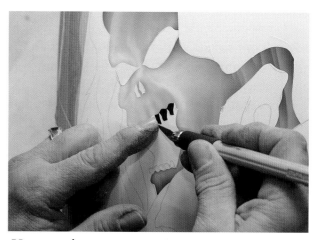

Upper teeth are next...

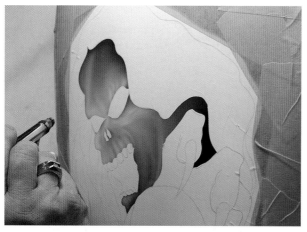

...and quickly an image emerges within the mask.

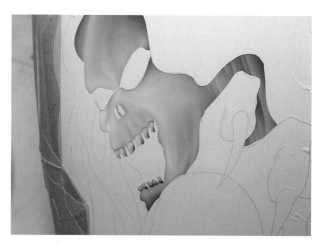

...note how much can be done using only one color of paint.

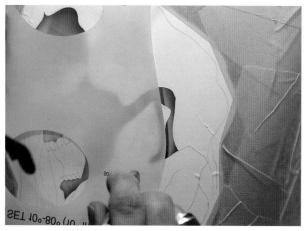

Though it's hard to see, the area being painted with the stencil will be hair, and the lines will work into the overall flow of the skull's mane.

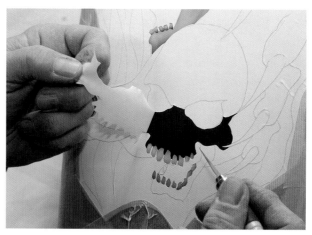

Work on the lower skull begins now.

Start with Highlights

The photos show how highlights done in white begin to define the upper brow, cheek bones and the area above the teeth. With these basic shapes established, Lenni begins to "pull the upper teeth," prior to painting these in the same basecoat white. Because he's working on a dark color, the white works with the underlying dark color to give definition to each feature.

After doing the teeth on the upper skull Lenni pulls the mask on the teeth belonging to the lower skull and paints in the highlights using the same white used all along. Next the mask for most of the lower face is pulled and the brow and cheek bones are painted in, much as was done on the upper skull. Once the basic shape of the lower skull is established, Lenni uses more white to detail the lower skull's lower jaw.

Q&A: Lenni Schwartz

Lenni, how about a little background?

I started as sign painter, pictorial artist and pinstriper. Airbrushing came in when I did airbrush letters, and when I wanted to create a chrome effect.

How about your airbrush and paint picks?

I use an Iwata Eclipse because it's light and maneuverable. It does anything I need from fine to large and it's dependable. I like bottles, because they make it easy to change colors and I don't need 12 airbrushes. For paint I like House of Kolor. It's user friendly, you can mix any color you want. Mostly I use their PBC and KBC lines. Not much candy.

Do you do body work and basecoats or just the art?

I just do the art, no basecoat and no clear, and no body work.

What's the hardest part of what you do?

Getting the depth and dimension I want. I do a pencil drawing first, and I take my time.

Any final words of wisdom?

Be patient, don't try to take the world on in one day. Be persistent and don't be afraid to try it out.

The painting progresses much as it did for the upper skull...

...with the brow line and cheekbones established first...

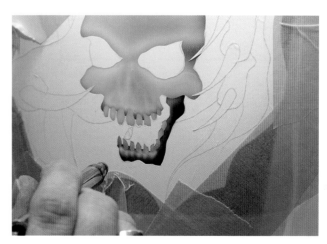

...followed by the teeth and lower jaw.

61

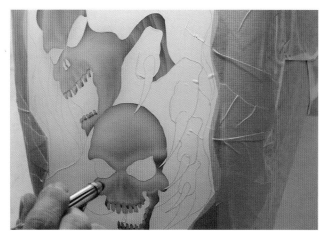

To give the skulls some color Lenni does a mist coat of sunset yellow...

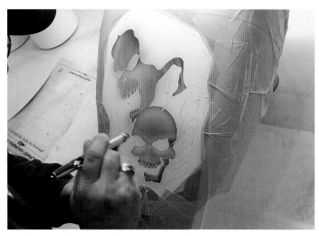

...followed by another of tangelo.

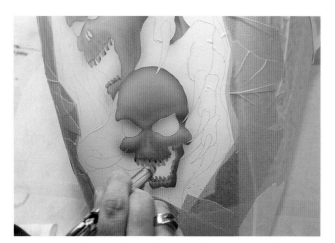

Violet pearl is used more sparingly, to create deeper shadows on select parts of the design.

Now Add Color

Up to this point, Lenni has only used one color, white. It's time now however, to liven things up with a bit of sunset yellow from H of K's PBC line. The yellow (PBC 31) is applied as an overspray, or mist coat over the entire image "just to begin giving it a little color" explains Lenni. The process of adding color continues as Lenni adds a second color, Tangelo (PBC 32) from the same PBC line, in the same way. The third color is violet pearl (PBC 40), applied only to the bottom of the shadows.

Though some airbrush artists change the speed of the reducer depending on the situation and amount of actual paint flowing through the airbrush, Lenni uses number 310, fast reducer, all the time. "I like to be fast," explains Lenni, "I want to tape on top of that paint right away."

After using the violet to darken the shadows, Lenni uses more white to go over all the highlights and the teeth again. He also uses the white to paint in cracks in the skulls.

Big Hairy Deal

With the basic faces and skulls established, Lenni pulls more of the mask covering the hair on the upper skull. As shown in the photos, these areas are painted in a series of passes that follow the basic flow of the hair.

The pattern continues, pull a few mask areas, paint them carefully in white, then pull another series of small masks and paint those areas. It's interesting to see how much more detail Lenni achieves in this way, rather than just pulling all the masks for the "hair" and painting the entire area at once.

To darken certain parts of the face including the chin of the upper skull, and better define some of the edges, Lenni uses basecoat black. For some of this work, like the chin, Lenni masks off nearby areas before applying any paint (see page 64).

The Hand

At this point much of the image is still covered by the original mask, in particular the claw (or hand) and the eye, both of which are now unmasked. Parts of the image, like the upper jaw and the lower skull, are back-masked before any

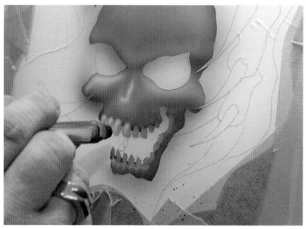

Back to white basecoat, used to create highlights on the teeth and certain raised parts of the skull.

The hair is painted in stages. After pulling a section of mask and painting the area with white streaks...

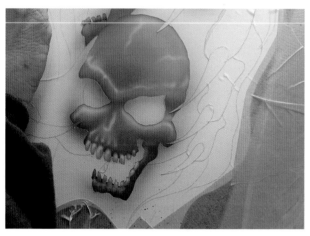

Progress shot shows the lower skull so far, with most of the prominent features established.

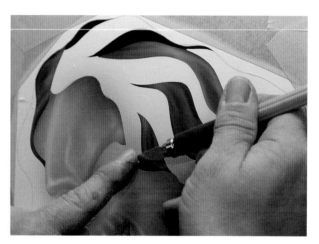

...another section of mask is pulled...

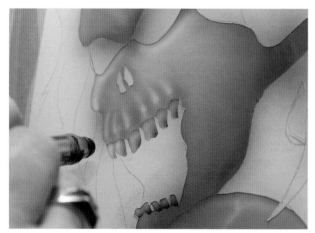

Before starting on the hair, Lenni uses more white to further brighten the teeth and raise the area above each tooth.

...and painted in the same fashion.

One section at a time, Lenni creates a wild head of hair, flowing and layered.

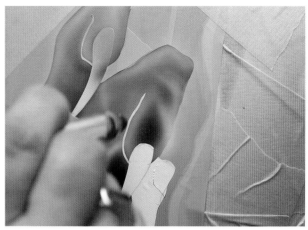

...which is used to establish the basic outline and highlights.

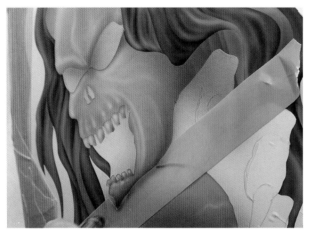

A temporary mask and light coats of basecoat black are used to darken and define the jaw line.

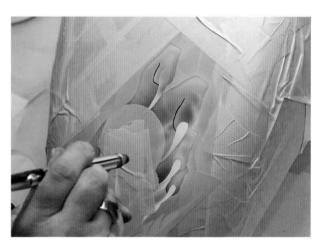

Everything needs to match, so the same color sequence used on the skulls is used on the hand as well...

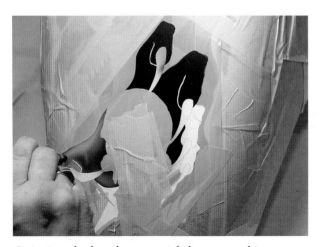

Painting the hand starts with basecoat white...

...sunset yellow, tangelo and then...

painting can begin. Once the painting can commence, it's more basecoat white. As was done with the skulls earlier, light coats of white are used to establish the basic contours of the hand, including the knuckles.

To help the hand match the "flesh tone" of the skulls, Lenni applies a series of mist coats, starting with sunset yellow, followed by tangelo and ending with violet pearl. Now the claws themselves are unmasked. The area nearby is masked off and the process starts over with basecoat white used, initially, to establish the highlights. For a little of the ghoulish factor, the tips of each claw are painted with ultra orange (PBC 64) followed by hot pink (PBC 39) Next, black is used to provide detail to the fleshy part of the hand around the claws

Because of the multiple layers of masking when Lenni pulls the tape, he had to be careful not to pull the masking paper underneath.

THE EYES HAVE IT

A good airbrush artist needs to think ahead. In the case of the eyes for the lower skull, Lenni paints these in flames because the lower part of the tank will be flamed later and this way the flames will seem to reach right up into the lower skull. The colors are sunset yellow, tangelo, ultra orange and a little black along the bottom.

The same basecoat black is used to outline areas like the eyes, teeth and claws, and to detail the upper and lower skull. The photos do a better job of explaining just how the detail work done at this point really brings the skulls to life.

FLAMES

After pulling all the remaining masking, Lenni starts his flames with white, applied in a series of passes to the area below the lower skull.

Yellow (PBC 31) is next, applied right on top of the white. Color number three is tangelo,

Continued on page 69

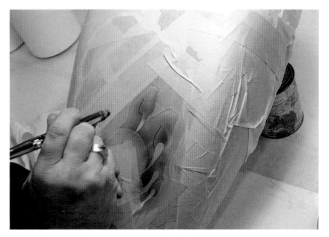

...violet pearl for dark, rich shadows.

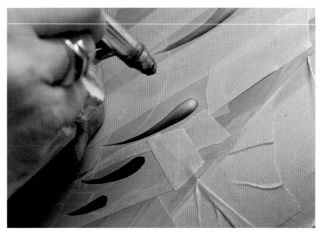

The claws are painted in white, after pulling the mask and back-masking the surrounding area.

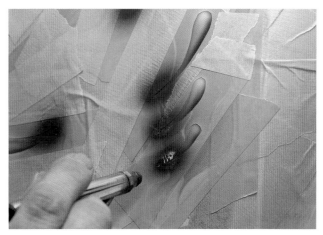

Ultra orange and hot pink create a nice red on the tip of each claw.

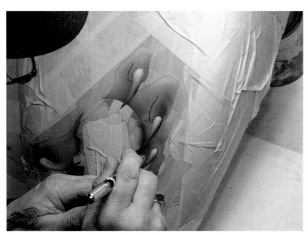

The final step in the creation of the claws is a little basecoat black.

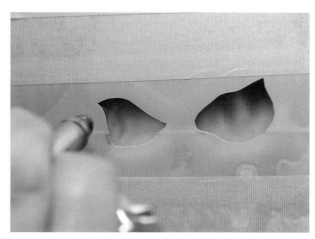

...next comes sunset yellow,...

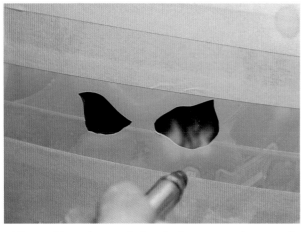

After pulling the mask for the lower set of eyes and back-masking the area nearby, Lenni starts a subtle set of reality flames.

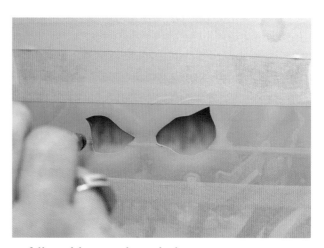

...followed by tangelo and ultra orange.

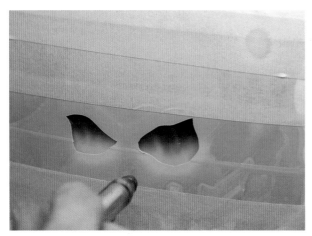

White is used first as a basecoat that will give the flames brilliance...

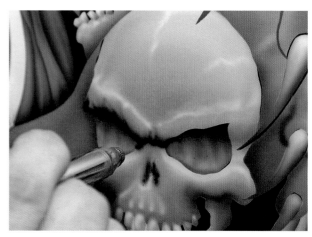

Outlined with black as the final step.

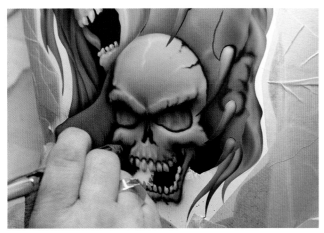

More black is used to detail the nose and eye sockets...

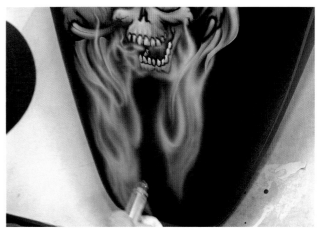

You can see the flame-shapes emerging from the white, the paint isn't put down all at once but in multiple light passes.

...and separate the two skulls from each other.

Sunset yellow is next...

A progress shot shows the two skulls nearly finished and ready for the next step.

...laid down on top of the licks already there.

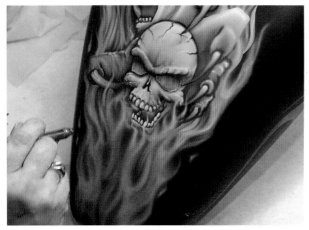

The yellow is followed by tangelo...

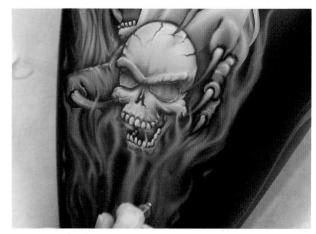

You can see the transition, how the flames are built step by step until all they need...

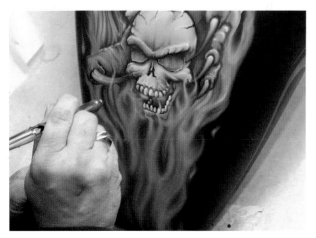

Which is laid down on top of the other two colors.

...is a little black to create hard edges.

Candy apple red is used to make the fire really red...

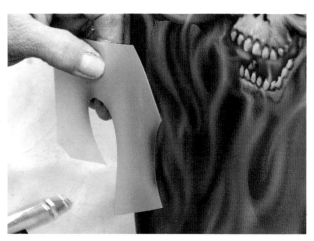

Which is why Lenni uses a stencil at this point.

sprayed (again) right on top of the white and yellow that are already there.

Next comes candy apple red basecoat, (KBC 11). Some of the passes with candy apple are tight and follow the flame shape closely, others are light mist coats designed to tint the whole area. Though black wouldn't seem like a flame color, Lenni uses a little basecoat black and a stencil (check the images on the facing page) to give the flames more definition. At the same time he adds more detail around the teeth and the outer edge of lower skull.

FINAL DETAILS

The little things do make a huge difference. With the flames finished, it's time to add shadings and outlines that help give the image definition. Cracks around the eye sockets are done with basecoat black. And just a minute later the same color is used to add details to upper jaw, on the upper skull, as well as to add the deep lines in the skull's face.

Though not shown in any of the photos, Lenni stops often during the painting to clean the airbrush.

1) The same black is used to detail the eye sockets...

2) ...and teeth.

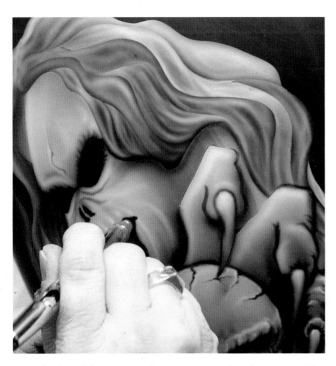
3) Black is likewise used to to create the deep wrinkles in the face...

4) ...and upper jaw that help make the skull look really aged and evil.

Lenni switches to white, to highlight the facial fissures and change the color of the hair.

The additional white changes the hair from soft and flowing to crazy and weird.

The evil-eye glimmer is done in two steps, first a pinpoint of white, followed by a little candy apple red (for an evil gleam) seen in the next image.

Note the highlights on each tooth, a good example of the detail required for truly good airbrush work.

Additional white is used to highlight the "nose"

White is used freehand to form the jagged lightening.

Before declaring the piece finished more white is used to add another layer, another dimension, to the hair on the upper skull. As Lenni says, "the hair really finishes him off." A spot of white is added to the eyes at the same time. A mist of candy apple red is then added to warm up the "skin tones" just a little, and to give the eyes in the upper skull a truly evil glow.

White is next, used in multiple steps to provide details to the teeth and parts of the face. Additional details like more wisps of hair and more highlights on the teeth, are also done before Lenni puts away the basecoat white (see the facing page).

LIGHTENING STRIKES

Like Frankenstein, these twin ghouls need a little electrical energy to give them life. Lenni starts the bolts of lightening as jagged lines of basecoat white, painted freehand and tinted with a little purple (PBC 65). Next comes more purple to give each bolt of lightening a stronger glow.

The final step is a little more yellow used to brighten the flames before the piece is officially declared finished.

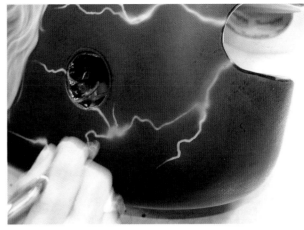

Then the bolts of lightening and the junctions are tinted with purple to very good effect.

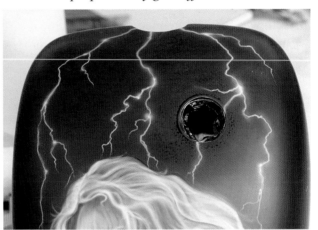

A progress shot shows the lightening raining down on the evil monster.

The best images are often a mixture of effects. Not just a set of flames or a skull, but an image that combines two skulls of slightly different styles with a set of flames licking up from underneath.

Chapter Five

Nick Pastura

Helmet Head

Shown here is the work of talented airbrush artist Nick Pastura of Cleveland, Ohio. Nick is best known for wild helmets, yet his resume' includes banners, signs and cover art for some very well-known bands, as well as more conven-tional airbrush work on vehicles of all types. If that weren't enough, Nick is very comfortable doing complete bike-builds, including all the metal, molding and paint work.

The project we chose for this chapter is one

The nearly finished helmet - a combination of orange and black scallops, and mechanical details like rivets, pivots, and seams.

of Nick's helmets, painted for NASCAR driver Jeff Burton "This guy, he likes silver riveted stuff," explains Nick. "The design is a graphic pattern similar to what's already on the car. And like most of the designs, this one came out of my head. Mostly people let me do what I want, I get to do my own thing most of the time."

BASE PAINT

The first two coats of paint are Dupont basecoat, silver effect (N9519K), followed by a taping sequence. "On this helmet I go straight to the tank without a sketch," adds Nick, "I just fly with it. With NASCAR helmets they need them so fast, they call on Monday afternoon and want them there on Tuesday."

Nick masks off a band that wraps around the helmet, marking it first with stabilo pen and then with fineline tape, finishing up with regular masking tape.

Before going farther, Nick wipes the helmet off with 3M Prep-Solvent 70, a water based prod-

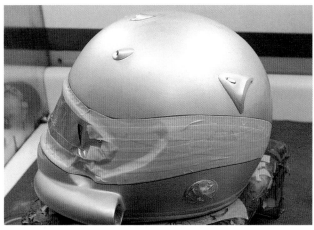

The project really starts as the white helmet is painted silver, then masked off through the middle.

Next comes two coats of orange...

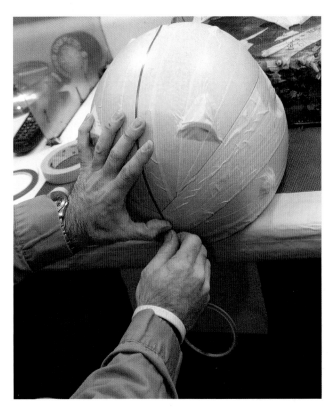

After the entire helmet is taped off, and before starting on the design, Nick creates a centerline with a piece of fineline tape.

...followed by more tape.

73

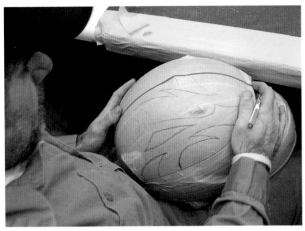

Nick draws out the designs right on the helmet, partly because of time constraints.

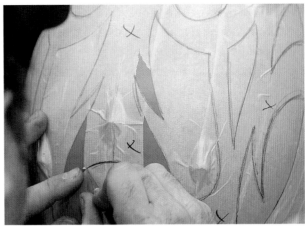

Tape is cut with an Xacto knife and then the design is pulled out.

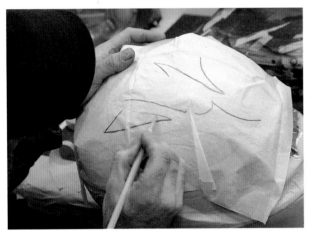

Once he has a design he likes, the next step is to trace that design onto a piece of paper.

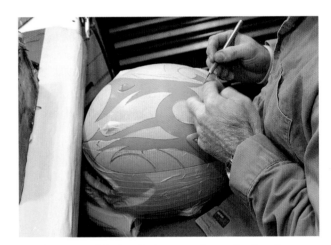

Nick's Xacto blades don't come from the lumber store. "I buy them at a craft store, they're half as much and twice as sharp."

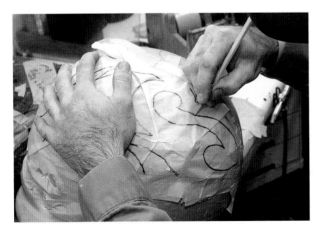

By flipping the paper over Nick has a perfect mirror image. As he runs over the design with a soft pencil, the pencil marks on the other side of the paper are transferred onto the helmet.

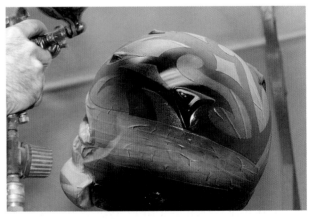

The black is applied in the booth, with a short wait between the first and second coat.

uct that he describes as, "a good cleaner that takes all the wax and grease off without touching the paint. You have to be sure to wipe it off wet though and not let it dry."

The second color to go down on the helmet is orange, specifically Dupont orange, (YS018K). At this point the entire helmet is taped off. Which seems odd, until you realize that Nick is a man with a plan.

Before going farther Nick marks a front to back centerline on the helmet in fineline tape, then begins to actually draw out the design right on the tape.

TRACING THE DESIGN

Nick makes a tracing of one side and uses that to duplicate the design on the other side. "You can use anything with a soft lead for tracing, " explains Nick. "Once I have the design on one half the helmet, I trace it off onto tracing paper, then flip it to get the mirror image on the other side. By going over the design with the same soft lead pencil used before, the pencil marks on the "inside" of the tracing paper are transferred to the tape.

"What's nice is I save the tracing paper when the job is done. So if he needs another helmet done quick I have the pattern." Finishing the design on the helmet does require some drawing by hand, especially along the lower edge and on the air intake.

START CUTTING

Using an Xacto knife Nick now begins cutting out the design he traced onto the helmet, with the warning that, "You have to decide which sections come out and which stay on the helmet, it's easy to make a mistake." The black basecoat goes on next in two coats and after a break it's time to pull the tape revealing an orange and black helmet.

PINSTRIPING

For the pinstriping Nick uses both a small lettering brush as well as a more typical natural-bristle pinstriping brush. And though most pinstripers "mix" the paint on a glossy magazine page, Nick simply puts a piece of masking tape

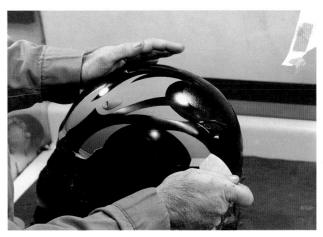

As the tape is pulled you can start to see the design emerge.

Next comes the pinstriping, done with a Mack number 00 brush and some...

...H of K lettering urethane (without any hardener).

Paint is mixed with H of K reducer to a good consistency. Sometimes Nick uses a lettering brush in lieu of the Mack pinstriping brush.

...apply it to the helmet.

Time to re-mask the helmet and start in on the next part of the job.

The little pre-cut stickies (available in various sizes) are used as a mask for the rivets.

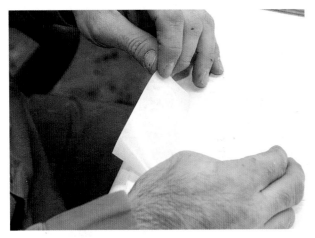

Transfer paper is used to pick up the logo and then...

With the various masks in place Nick starts in with the first coat of black, "mixed twice as thin as normal."

on the bench and mixes on that. The paint itself is blue (U 99) urethane striping paint from H of K reduced with their special reducer (U 00) intended specifically for this particular lettering paint.

LOGOS AND RIVETS

Before proceeding with the application of the logos and some decorative rivets, Nick masks off the outer edge of the silver section. Cingular logos are cut out on Frisket paper, Nick picks each one up with a piece of transfer paper and positions it on the sides of the helmet.

For the rivets, Nick uses the little pre-cut adhesive backed stickies, shown in the photos. These are available at a variety of office stores, including Office Max.

Nick starts by spraying basecoat black along the inside of the logo's perimeter, and on top of each rivet-mask. In the case of the rivets, Nick creates a little "run" coming down off the rivet. With additional black paint applied outside, Nick essentially "shadows" the logo to make it stand up off the surface.

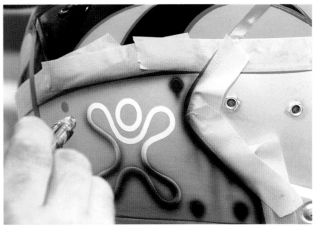

The logos are outlined in a series of steps, using an Iwata Eclipse airbrush....

...the effect is to create a 3-D effect for the Cingular logo.

To add a seam along the side of the helmet, Nick first makes a tape line and then comes in with black paint.

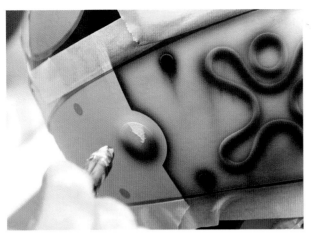

To make a large rivet, or hinge, Nick starts with a big pre-cut circle or mask. After adding a black shadow he starts on the upper highlight.

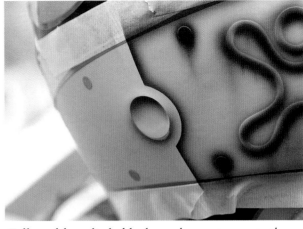

Followed by a little black on the top to create the effect seen here.

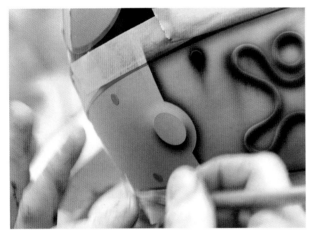

Then the mask comes off...

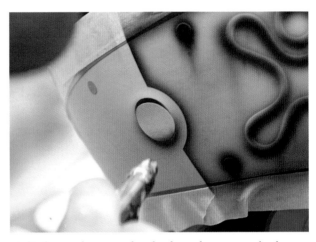

A little touch up to the shadowed area on the bottom and the deal is done.

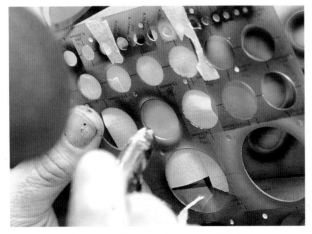

The stencil is moved into place and Nick sprays white on the lower part of the stenciled area.

After shading and shadowing the logo and rivets on the side of the helmet, all of the masking material is pulled off.

White then Black then White.....

The short sequence shown on the facing page is a good example of the multiple steps necessary to create a believable rivet. Starting with a pre-cut mask, Nick applies a black shadow on the bottom and then a white highlight on the top. After pulling off the mask, Nick uses a stencil and more white paint to create a highlight on the lower part of the rivet. With the mask off you can see the effect of the multiple steps. The only thing missing is a little more shadow along the bottom, created with black paint after re-applying the pre-cut mask.

Time now to pull the logo tape (bottom right of the facing page) and the small pre-cut masks for the rivets. Nick's next step is a little bit of black shadow added to the center of each rivet.

A Vent for Hot Air

Creating a very mechanical helmet doesn't end with rivets and seams. A screened vent seems like a good idea, added to the back of the helmet.

Step one is the application of multiple pieces of tape placed on the helmet in the shape of a shallow V. Step two is to mask off the V. Before any paint is applied Nick tapes a piece of screen across the vent's opening. The black sprayed through the screen creates a "screen" in the back

Working by hand without a stencil, Nick adds a shadow to the center of each rivet.

A progress shot shows the incredible detail created with the careful use of only two colors.

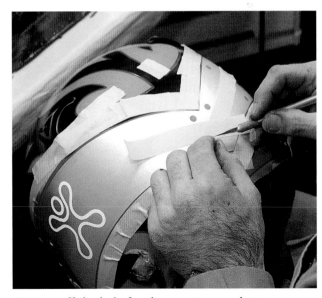

Taping off the hole for the vent is a multi-step process.

After the vent is taped off Nick positions a screen over the area.

Black paint is sprayed through a mask to create...

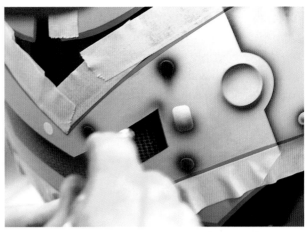

And also adds details, like this shadow, to the vent.

...a very believable vent in the back of the helmet.

The small rectangular shapes are created much like the rivets, using a pre-cut mask as the starting point, followed by a shadow and highlight.

With the same black in the airbrush, Nick starts on another series of rivets...

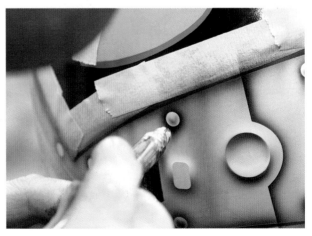

Each rivet requires the creation of two separate shadows and then a highlight.

of the helmet. The only thing missing is a shadow added at the top and then the tape can be pulled.

More Rivets and Shapes

The end of the project includes more of the little details that separate a really good graphic from all the rest. Things like shadows at the corners of the vent and under the small rivets, done freehand with the brush held very close to the helmet

To add an additional detail and to help separate the two major parts of the helmet Nick does a very thin black pinstripe where the silver meets the orange.

Now he adds a few rivets on the side (not shown) and works his way across the front of the helmet, adding additional seams and rivets as he goes.

With careful shading Nick is able to continue the seams up all the way to the black pinstripe (note the photo on the right of this page).

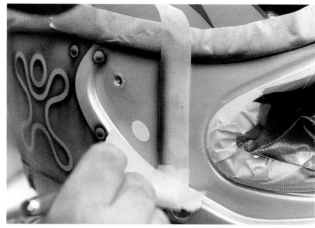

More mechanical detail is added here, in the form of another rivet, and a seam.

With the rivet-mask still in place Nick applies black paint.

The logos added late in the process were done in this simple manner - use the logo as a mask and paint the center in by hand.

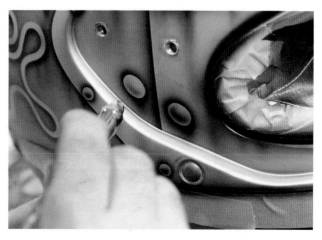

Then pulls the mask and creates the second shadow.

To create one more Cingular logo without having to do any real masking, Nick simply picks up a logo with transfer paper, applies it to the orange part of the helmet, and fills the area inside the logo with black paint, working by hand with a small brush.

What's left is a little clean up, done with a gray scotch-brite pad and water, and the final clearcoat.

Close up shows the intricate shading that makes the logos and rivets stand up off the surface.

The overall design is just what Nick described at the beginning of the project: A graphic that matches the car and uses lots of rivets and silver riveted stuff.

Q&A: Nick Pastura

Where did you learn your craft?

It was working for an advertising agency and they laid a bunch of people off. I started doing professionally what I did as a hobby. I didn't want to collect unemployment. That was in the early 1990s. I have no art training other than high school.

How did you learn how to use an airbrush?

I'm self taught. I didn't even read a book or anything. And at the time there wasn't a lot information out there. I just did it by the seat of my pants. I jumped in full speed, both airbrush and pinstripe. I was already doing paint and body work so I understood fillers and paints. So I set up shop at my mom's house, hot rods mostly to start with. I look back on it now and I think it was just meant to be.

How'd you get into painting helmets?

I painted one for a local racer because he was a friend. He went to Daytona, put it on the roof of the car, Earnhardt Jr. saw it and asked where it came from. Jr. called and then it snowballed from there. Simpson, the helmet company saw it and they recommended me and that really helped.

Anything that's special about painting helmets?

Make sure the preparation is good, get into all the nooks and crannies. 320 grit is what I use for the final sanding. I saw this as an avenue to incorporate advertising into the helmet, so I got more intricate with designs, no one else was doing that. The compound curves are hard, it's hard to make letters look straight for example. It just took time until I learned how to do that.

What about paint?

I use both PPG and Dupont. I stay with their brand of reducers, mix and match will cause you trouble some day.

And airbrushes?

I use Iwata, the most versatile airbrush on the market. They are good workhorses. I like the bottles, it's fast and easy and I can grab them quick.

Where do your ideas come from?

Books, magazines, TV, Disney. Everywhere I go I'm looking for something. I might look at a label in the grocery store and get an idea. I'm always, always looking.

How much of the overall work do you do?

I do the basecoat all the way to clear, it gives me more control. If there's a mistake I know where to look. You know there's not going to be a paint reaction because you know which paint you're painting over. And you're not waiting for the guy who's doing the basecoat to finish.

Advice?

If you really want to try something, just pick up and try it. Go to places where people are doing what you want to do. I used to stand at hot rod events and watch the pinstripers. Buy books.

Don't be afraid to ask for advice from the paint jobber or other artists, most of them, if they love what they do, will give you good advice.

Nick Pastura, master of many skills.

Chapter Six

Mathew Willoughby

Details, Details, Details

These pages contain the work of Mathew Willoughby from New Middletown, Ohio. Matt is quick to point out the fact that, "I'm not a very fast artist." What he forgets to mention however, is the incredible amount of detail his go-slow approach allows. Matt's art is detailed to the point where it very nearly takes a magnifying glass to truly see all the lines, shadows and shadings. Though motorcycle work makes up the main part of Matt's work, he also does a fair amount of com-

"I like this design because it's very bright and colorful, but still classic and somewhat conservative."

mercial work (both airbrush painting, and pure design and concept work).

Like most artists, Matt starts the project seen here with a sketch, "but the sketch is only a guide," explains Matt. "I do the layout right on the tanks, because that way I don't have trouble with the sketch fitting the tank and the way it wraps around the corners."

The design is "drawn out" on the side of the tank using thin masking tape. When he's finally happy with it ("the layout is the slowest part of the whole job") Matt makes a tracing and then flips it over to create a mirror-image layout for the other side. To trace the outline of the art onto the other side, Matt slides a piece of Saral paper (check the photos) under the tracing paper and goes over the tracing with a pencil. Before getting too involved in the second image, he has to make sure not only that it matches the original, but also that it is positioned the same on the second tank as it is on the first.

"I like this Saral paper," explains Matt, "it's water based, non toxic and doesn't affect the paint, though I do wipe the lines off later." Once the design is transferred to the other tank most of the tank is masked off prior to the first round of painting.

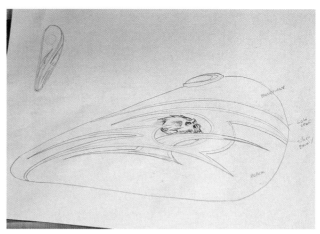

Matt uses the initial sketch as a way to flesh-out his design ideas...

...the layout is done right on the tank itself.

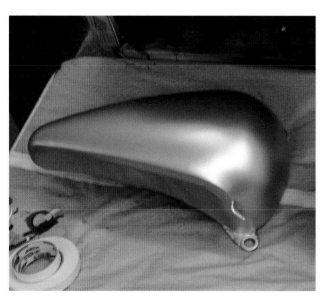

The bare tank, with only the basecoat and a coat of SG 100 clear.

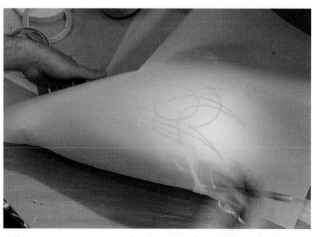

Then a tracing is made that can be used to duplicate the design on the other side.

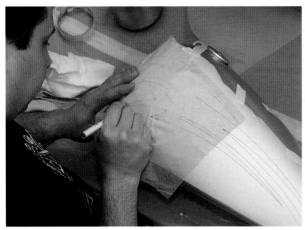

Here you can see the blue Saral paper positioned under the tracing paper. Think of it as carbon paper for art work.

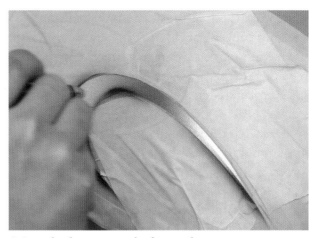

More shadowing on the big arch.

Everything is masked off except two of the main spears...

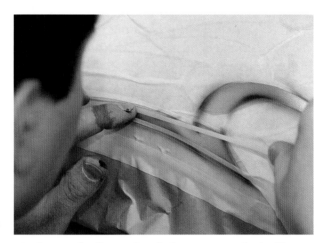

And now the future beveled area is masked off.

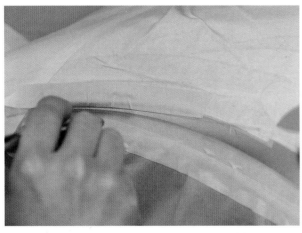

...which are shadowed with transparent black.

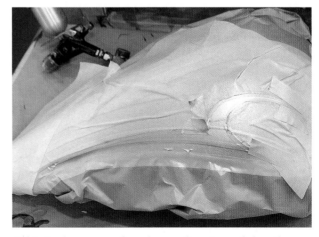

This is the spear after the application of the silver-blue paint.

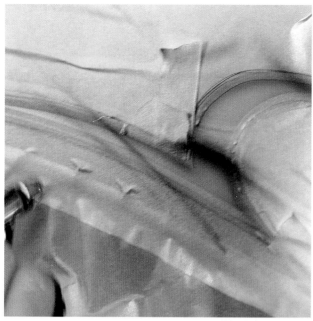

Next, the highlight areas are streaked with black, after pulling the fineline tape that masked off the beveled area.

START PAINTING

The first light applications of paint are done with specially mixed transparent black. Matt creates this hue by mixing House of Kolor black basecoat with SG 100 clear, over-reduced a little. The shadow areas of the two main spears are the first to receive paint. Next he puts a thin line of tape down over the shadow, "only because that will be the bevel," explains Matt.

Next Matt puts down a little silver, but he doesn't want to use the same silver that covers the rest of the tank. The idea is to create a little contrast between the two colors. "I mix a little blue in with the silver to give it a slightly different color," explains Matt.

Streaks of black come next, "this helps to give it that metallic look," explains Matt, followed by more shadows on the upper part of the spear.

THE PATTERN REPEATS

After pulling the tape and back-masking part of the design, Matt starts another series of shadows on the new unmasked area. The second sequence, like the first, is done in a series of steps, complete with the use of thinline tape to create a beveled edge and the application of more silver-blue paint.

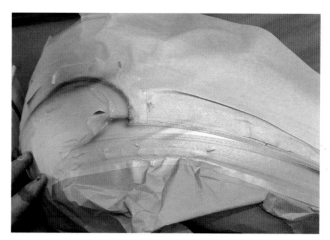

Before pulling the tape Matt adds a shadow on the highlight side of the spear and some subtle streaks farther back on the tank.

Black shadows are added at the edge of the area Matt just untaped. "You have to wipe off the blue lines, or they get painted over and you can't get them off."

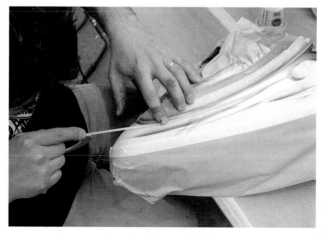

Now another beveled edge is taped off with thin fineline tape.

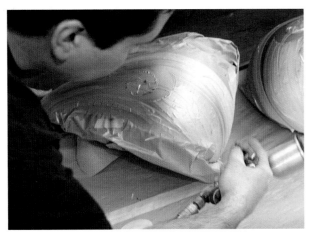

Two coats of silver-blue are applied to the area shown.

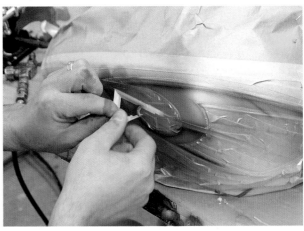

Pulling tape, "I always try to avoid cutting on the sheet metal, you end up with a cut line in the paint and it gives you trouble later."

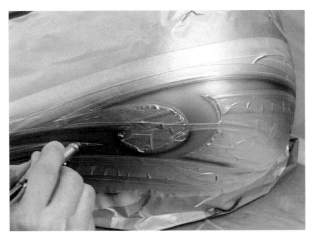

Next, the edges are shadowed with a light application of black paint.

More details, in the form of additional black streaks, are added now.

Highlights are added with silver, rather than white paint.

After masking off the art work on the upper part of the tank, Matt sprays the bottom half in black.

The skull mask is cut out over the light table.

The design is fairly complex and requires that Matt keep track of each step in the process. As he explains, "You have to be able to see the whole thing in your head before you start, You can't just make it up as you go."

After allowing the second coat of silver-blue to dry Matt does another set of streaks with transparent black. For highlights Matt uses silver, explaining as he does, "I don't use white on silver for highlights because compared to the silver the white looks dull, almost gray."

MORE MASKING AND A NEW STENCIL

Before masking off the upper art work Matt adds a few more black streaks. After masking off the upper art work the bottom of the tank is painted black. The small skull in the center of the tank starts as a sketch which is then used to create a stencil as shown in the nearby photos.

"I tried to create a skull shape that works with the shape of the graphic," says Matt.

With the stencil of the skull in place, Matt

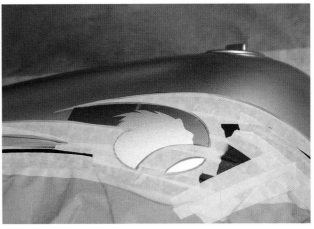

The outer part of the skull stencil is set in place first, only to help position the main part of the stencil. The outer part will be removed later.

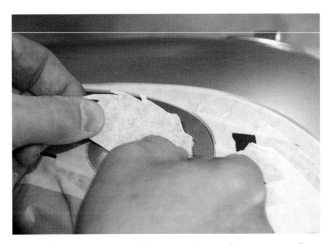

Now the main part of the stencil can be positioned correctly.

Some areas of the stencil are cut out and others are just "windows" that can be opened and closed.

Q&A: Matt Willoughby

Matt, how about some background?

I went into the sign business out of high school. In 1986 I started traveling with Steve (Steve Wizard) to shows. Then three years later I went to another sign studio where we restored old carousel horses. I still did shows on weekends with Steve, that would be 1990. Then I started doing major shows and painting bikes. I worked for Steve full time for a while, but I've been on my own since 1996.

Tell us a little more about the carousel horses and how that affects your current work.

I like the gold work and the history of the scroll work, it was a good experience. I got to do a lot of pinstriping and learn from a very talented crew.

Is most of your work motorcycle work?

Yes, 80% is motorcycle work, I do some automotive concept drawing, commercial work illustrating with Illustrator and Photoshop.

What are your paint choices and why?

Spies Hecker and H of K, because the H of K candies and pearls can't be duplicated. Spies because of the quality and durability. German clears are more resilient. If you stick your thumbnail in a clear, it leaves an imprint, it doesn't get as brittle. You can buff later, get fewer stone chips. The bases have no window for adhesion, you can paint it and then clear it a year later. It's more expensive, but I think you actually use less so it comes out about the same.

Your airbrush choice and why?

Iwata HP, because of the consistency. You can get fine detail and they handle the heavy urethanes. I put an illustrator needle in a automotive airbrush. For base paints I use SATA HVLP guns but for candies I use a conventional gun.

Do you do all the work, the mud the candy and the clear?

For the prep, metal and mud work I rely on both my brother-in-law Jonathan Fragosa, and my brother Troy Willoughby. I figured out I can't do it all myself. After they're done I start with 2-1/2 coats of primer, then block it so I know it's flat and then take it the rest of the way. The candies and clears are part of my work too. I usually clear twice with a day between to dry. I sand with 800 after the first coat and then do the second coat and then buff.

You use a lot of what might be called tattoos, how did that evolve?

I like the subtlety of designs like that after they are candied, I think the artwork shouldn't be the main thing that you see when you look at the bike, the art work should compliment the design of the bike.

Where do you get ideas?

Everywhere not just bike magazines, but tattoo magazines,flash art, a lot of jewelry designs, deco designs, I try to draw from a lot of sources.

Any advice to other painters?

You need endurance. It doesn't happen overnight. I like working on the bikes, I like the industry. My favorite design is a nice clean flame job. I enjoy the people who build bikes, they're having fun and you get to deal with people when they're at their best.

Surrounded by what might be called his PhD thesis, Matt Willoughby is a man who always goes the extra mile for detail.

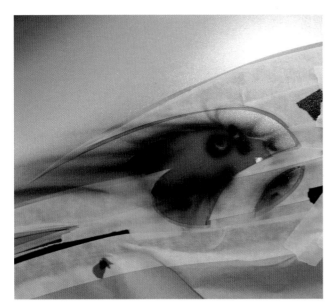

The streaks are added to the area surrounding the skull - giving it the look of a crazy professor.

Matt starts on the eyes first...

...recesses in the skull are created by pulling back a window and applying black paint.

Once the skull is mostly finished, Matt can pull the stencil.

pulls out the details like the eyes and nose. The eyeballs are painted in first, with black, which will be candied later.

Black streaks are added to the skulls with the stencil still in place. Matt keeps the two tanks close to each other so he can compare the two images, "they won't be exact copies," explains Matt, "but they should be consistent."

For an image as small as the skull, Matt takes great care with all the shading and details. Even after doing the eyes, he peels back small windows (as shown) and applies black. These windows include things like the cavity on the side of the head, as well as the eyebrows.

A Streamline Hair-Do

To make what Matt call the "streamline hair-do," he uses small stencil and short bursts of black paint to create a repeating pattern on the skull. "When I'm working like this," adds Matt, "I always make sure the edges and details are sharp enough to show up under the candy that comes later."

Once the hair is pretty much finished, Matt adds more shadows and details to the skull working freehand. Before moving on to the next part of the project a shadow is added to the main spear

Matt uses a small stencil to create the streamline hair-do.

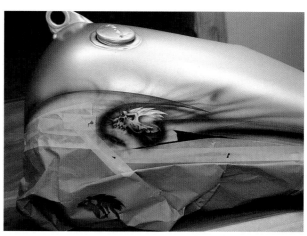

At this point Matt has pulled the tape on top and added a few final details to the skull.

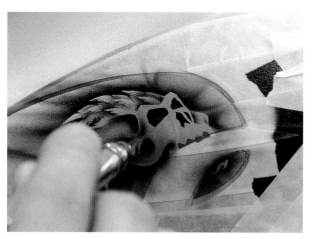

Many of the subtle shadings are done freehand.

After determining the width and shape of the silver leaf and the spear, Matt makes a tracing so the shapes can be duplicated on the other tank.

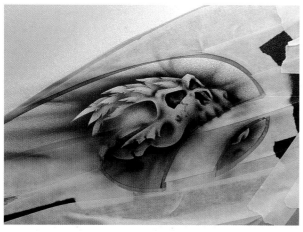

A progress shot shows a very detailed skull with features that help it to blend in with the rest of the design.

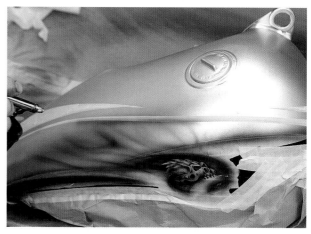

Matt adds the shadow for the silver spear before creating the spear itself.

"to give it good definition," and additional streaks of black are added to the tank where it's most curved. "That curved part is where the candy will be the hottest," explains Matt, "so it's nice to put something there."

SILVER LEAF AND UPPER SPEARS

To say that the layout for the top of the tank includes spears and a stripe of silver leaf is to understate the complexity of the design. First Matt does a multi layered tape-out of the spears as shown on the facing page, and adds shadows before creating the spears themselves, "The shadow will help give it dimension, help to make it interesting." Next, the tape is pulled off in layers and each layer painted a different shade of transparent black "I try to mask in layers," explains Matt, "so I can do the shadows around the main spear for example, and then pull the outer tape and get to the main image without having to go back and re-mask."

When all this work is finished the spears are taped off, leaving only the thin tapered area that will be covered in silver leaf. "I want the leaf to be wider at the front," explains Matt, "and the whole thing should taper to the back, helping to streamline the design."

The size is mixed with One-Shot "so you can gauge the coverage," (note the caption on the lower right). Matt unmasks the area immediately, "so we don't have any film build at the edge. The application of the sizing should be pretty generous," explains Matt, "other wise you get voids where the leaf won't adhere. You have to be careful not to touch it and then touch the tank, if you transfer sizing to other parts of the tank those areas will catch the gold leaf. Sometimes the leaf doesn't want to lie down, you have to breath on it to soften it and then press it down into the sizing"

STICK IT DOWN

"You need to be sure all the leaf is stuck down before you start running over it or burnishing it," explains Matt. "If you burnish it too soon you tear off little pieces and when you have to patch the leaf - and you can always tell later."

Matt pulls another layer of tape on the upper spear prior to spraying in another dark area.

Note how the shading gives the upper spear dimension and helps to set it up off the tank.

Silver leaf is next. First the area is sprayed with size, mixed with One-Shot (same base as the sizing) catalyzed with KU 100 (just enough to get it to harden before the clear goes on) with just a little reducer (turpentine) to make it flow through the gun.

"You have to let size dry until you get a 'whistling tack,' you can drag your knuckle across without leaving an imprint, but soft enough that your knuckle drags. It makes a whistle as you do it."

"Once the excess is torn off and it's stuck down good I can burnish it with another piece of cotton, moving it the long way."

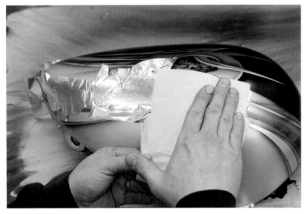

Each sheet is applied with modest but steady pressure - once the size has set up enough. Silver leaf comes in 5X5 inch sheets while gold comes in 3X3 inch sheets.

By spinning the tool shown here, Matt is able to create a subtle "engine turned" effect in the long silver spear.

A good bond is ensured by careful and gentle pressure applied with a cotton ball.

To help separate the silver-foil area from the rest of the tank Matt lays down a single black pinstripe on either side of the area.

Once it's stuck down with lots of individual dabs of cotton, Matt starts to run the cotton the long way, softly, per the photos on the left. "At this point you don't want to put anything over the silver until it's cleared," says Matt. "Not chemicals or finger prints or anything." Before going any further Matt wipes off the rest of the tank with Prepsol, to eliminate any dust from the foil.

THE PINSTRIPE AND FINAL DETAILS

The almost-final-step is to pinstripe the leaf. Matt does this with black (UO 1) paint from H of K, without any catalyst, reduced with H of K reducer (U 00). "One thing I don't like about leaf," says Matt, "you have to use a bigger pinstripe line that I usually do, just because you have to cover that rough edge."

Matt figures there's time for a few more details, done with a mechanical pen, a great tool for extra, tight detail. As Matt says, "It's especially good in areas where I want really good edge definition." The mechanical pen is filled with ink, "but it's not completely light fast," explains Matt, "so you have to be sure the clear you use has good UV protection. And they're water based so you have to clear them with something like SG 100 or it's too easy to just wipe them off with a wax and grease remover by accident.

The final step is three coats of candy brandy-wine (UK 01), and of course the clearcoats.

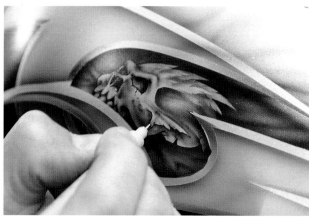

Matt adds new details, like a crack in the skull, and reinforces details already there with a more defined outline. The mechanical pen is a Pigma Micron.

The finished tank before the application of the candy.

I like to stay with a clear from the same manufacturer as the candy or topcoat. So in this case I used UC 35 clear from H of K. First two coats, then block sand and another two coats. The final step is buffing with McGuire's products.

Chapter Seven

Keith Hanson

Throw Out The Rules

Best known as the graphics artist for bike-builder Dave Perewitz, Keith Hanson is a man with a fresh approach. After nearly thirty years doing pinstripes, airbrush and paint work, Keith likes to disregard the rules of convention. Don't ask him how he gets the two sides of the tank exactly the same, because he doesn't even try. "Each piece is different," explains Keith. "It gives you a reason to go and look at the other side. I try to balance one side with the other,

Keith Hanson has his own ideas about graphic design. One of which is the idea that the right and left sides of a motorcycle tank do not have to be identical. In fact, Keith often works to ensure the two sides are similar in a design sense, but not even close to being the same.

you can do that by using up about the same amount of space on one side as the other, or you can use color for that. If the graphic is brighter on one side than the other, I might use a real bright pinstripe on the other side." And if you wonder why some of his pinstripes look so much like gold leaf, it's because they are gold leaf.

THE INITIAL LAYOUT

Rather than work from a sketch, Keith works out the design right on the tank, explaining as he does, "I tend to just do it, because if I think too much about the art I get too tight."

With the green basecoat already finished and sanded, the layout evolves right on the tank, done with green fineline tape. The layout takes time, each side needs to flow with a similar design. The next step is to cut out the overlapping pieces of tape.

The rest of the masking is done with wide masking tape cut out with the Xacto knife, then more tape and masking paper.

The layout is done directly on the tank, working without a sketch and without much in the way of preconceived ideas.

The design flows from Keith's head to his hands.

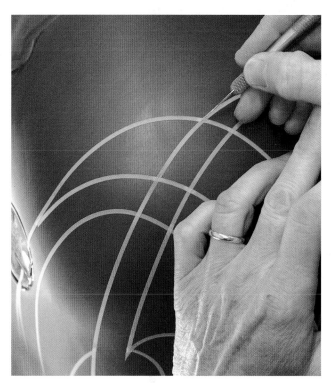

Before the actual masking can take place Keith cuts out the overlapping fineline tape.

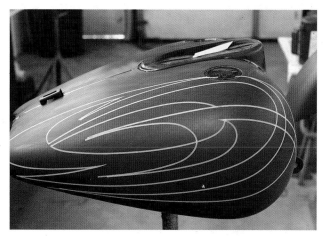

Here the outline of the graphic appears on the tank. The two sides will be "balanced" but not identical.

Once the design is finished, the masking is done with wide tape...

The light pink goes on first in two light coats.

...and paper.

Once the basecoat is dry Keith starts with hot pink, applied as streaks or a series of passes using the airbrush.

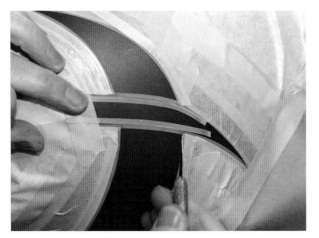

You have to know which spear goes over or under. In this case the horizontal spear goes over, which is why the 2 outer pieces of tape will be pulled off.

Passion pearl is next, sprayed on top of the hot pink to darken the streaks.

START SMALL

"I start with the smallest graphic," says Keith. "The one with the least amount of color in it. By doing the smallest areas first, it keeps me moving faster. Smaller areas dry faster and can be taped over faster, so I can move onto the next step quickly. During layout you have to be sure to modify the tape out where one spear runs under the other so you get the right effect."

The first color Keith applies is PPG light pink basecoat (DBC51589) applied to the entire spear in two coats. This is the base for the darker colors to follow. One of Keith's rules is to start light and go darker.

A PROGRESSION OF COLORS

In this case hot pink pearl from House of Kolor (PBC 39) is the first accent color applied over the light pink. The hot pink is applied in a series of passes, (note the photos). Keith explains that, "I like to flush the airbrush with reducer between each of the colors to ensure each color doesn't get mixed in with the previous color."

"As you go along with the project, applying various colors, you apply a little less of each color in the progression. In this case, passion pearl (PBC 65) is the second color. If the first color is 50%, the passion pearl is 30% and the final color is 20%."

Blue intensifier from PPG (DMX 220) is color number three. Sticking with Keith's plan of applying less and less paint with each step, the white is applied last, in a series of small, running highlights. To protect his airbrush work Keith applies two coats of DBC 500 intercoat clear using a SATA pistol-grip airbrush. This brush is bigger than most airbrushes but still smaller than a touch up gun.

"I always pull the tape carefully," explains Keith, "so I don't pull tape underneath that I would like to leave in place. Usually by the time I have the tape pulled the paint I've just done is dry enough to tape over and I can move right along with the project."

This is the panel after the blue intensifier (the last, and darkest, color) is added to the streaks.

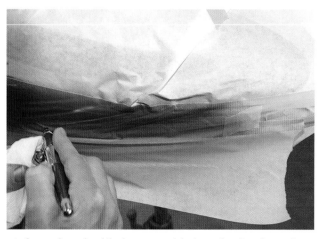

A few white highlights are added as the final touch...

...and the work can be unmasked.

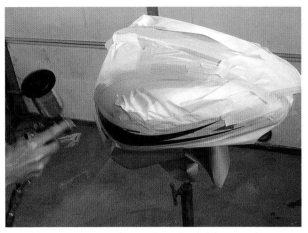

Another spear, another color, dark lilac in this case.

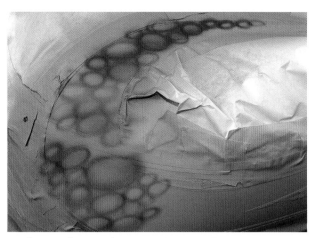

...then in hot pink (BC 39)...

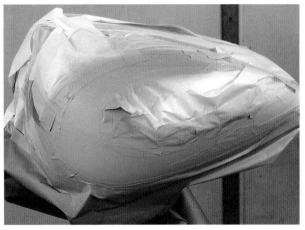

Two coats of the dark lilac are followed by green blue (DBC 17709) on the front of the spear.

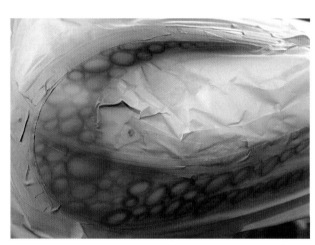

...which is darkened by blue intensifier (DMX 220)...

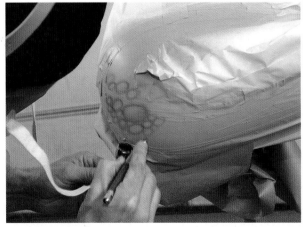

Abstract circles come next, done first in light pink pearl (PBC 57)...

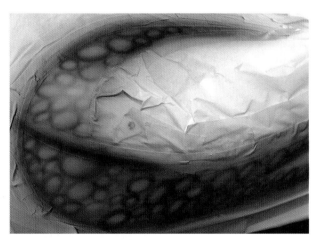

...and then a little black (DBC 1683).

Retape and Start Anew

After retaping, the next spear is coated first with dark lilac, (DBC 51598), applied with a touch up gun to the entire spear. Next, comes green blue (DBC 17709) applied in a series of small passes at the front of the area.

Light pink pearl (PBC 57) is next. This color is used to create a series of small circles. Sometimes Keith keeps the gun close for tight lines and detail, other times he moves it farther away for a softer edge.

Hot pink pearl (PBC 39) is next, used to create more circles surrounding those already there. These are created at random, with no apparent pattern. Blue intensifier, the darkest color of this series, is used to tone some of the circles already created and help to give them dimension. Black is next, used to darken some of the circles and to create a shadow line along the top of the spear.

Keith applies pearl (PPG PRL 89 mixed with DBC 500 intercoat clear and reduced 1:1) over the black to soften it a little bit (all references to black are DBC 1683). White highlights come next. Keith explains that, "these precise little pinpoints of white are used to separate the surfaces from the background."

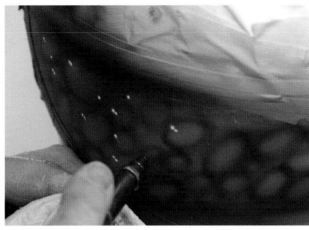

Small white highlights help to create the 3-D effect by making the highlight seem like it's the highest point...

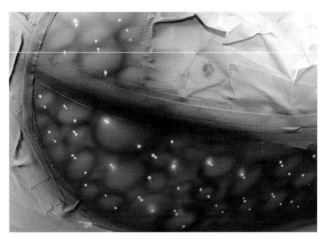

...the paint that catches the light.

...Keith begins to re-mask and prepare for another series of colors.

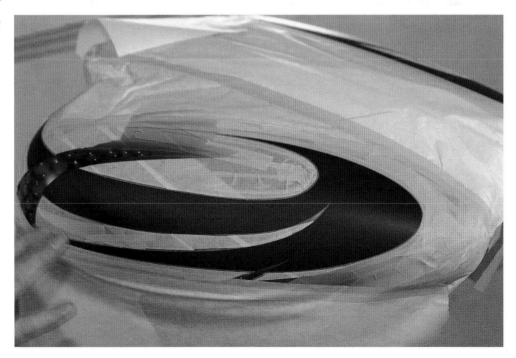

"I like to run 35 to 40 psi at the gun, and the same for the airbrushes."

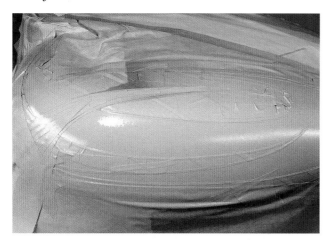

The biggest part of the design is the brightest, seen here after 3 coats of sunburst yellow.

"The white creates the illusion that the light is reflecting off the part that is closest to you. Again I moved from dark to light, and even though we didn't use very much white, look at the effect it has. After the white is finished I apply two more coats of intercoat clear to protect all this work."

THE MOST IMPORTANT AREA

"This progression is working really well," explains Keith. "Now we're at the biggest part of the design, the largest area and the one that will have the most color. It's more efficient to work this way. As I work I don't worry too much about the edges. A lot of these don't have to be perfect, you're going to have a pinstripe to cover any roughness."

Work on this next area starts with sunburst yellow (DBC 83032). The yellow is applied to the entire area in three light coats using a touch up gun. Sunrise pearl (PBC 30) is next, applied in two light coats, used in this case to tone and richen the sunburst yellow.

THE NEXT DESIGN

What might be called the accent colors start with sunset pearl (PBC 31), applied with an airbrush to the perimeter of the area, and in subtle streaks that follow the overall shape of the spear.

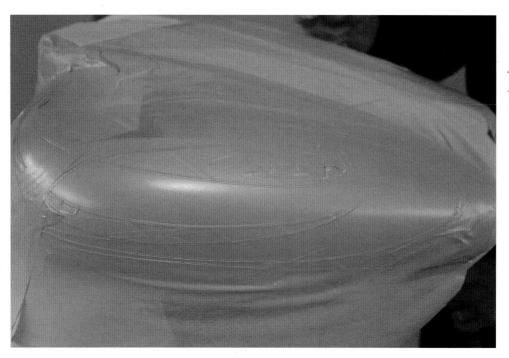

Sunrise pearl is applied on top of the sunburst yellow. The combination produces a totally new, and much richer, color.

Q&A: Keith Hanson

Keith, how did you get started doing airbrush work?

I remember the moment I developed a fascination with paint. I was seven years old and my sisters were starting a fan club. They needed a sign and I asked if they would let me work on it. My dad was artistic. That isn't how he made his living, but he always encouraged my artistic endeavors. My mom wanted me to go to art school, but I hated school so much that I couldn't see that. I didn't really start doing art work professionally until I was about 23. I've been on my own since 1978.

I started out pinstriping as a hobby and then it progressed. People say if you can stripe you can letter, so I started doing sign work. Then they started to ask, "Can you do gold leaf?" When they would ask about some skill I didn't have, I would go practice and then take the job.

I came into contact with motorcycles through a local painter John Hartnett. Many of the people I met then are still customers and friends, including, and especially, Dave Perewitz. I learned as I went along. The equipment, the paints and all the rest. For about nine years I painted and lettered funny cars, dragsters and show cars. Of course I did motorcycles too. But at one point I decided to switch, to work on motorcycles instead of race cars.

Where do you get your ideas?

I try to come up with new ideas so my work isn't so repetitive, I don't go to bike magazines for my ideas, that's the last place I look. I get a lot of ideas from the fashion industry, they are in the business of making you buy things you don't need. I like to look at their textures, their use of color.

The idea for the "circles" used on this tank came from a stone wall, that's where it started and look how far it's gone.

How do you pick colors and designs?

I let the design tell me what it's going to be, I don't pick colors ahead of time.

Which paints do you use?

I use H of K and PPG both, almost interchangeably. I don't use any water-based paints.

Which airbrush do you like?

My work horse airbrush is a Paasche VL 1. For more detail I use a Richpen 213C. To get automotive paints to go through the airbrush the paint needs to be over reduced by about 50%.

Talented and innovative, Keith Hanson is the only motorcycle guy to subscribe to both Cosmopolitan and Easyriders.

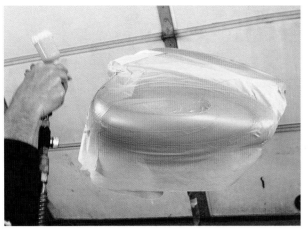

You can see the design develop as Keith applies swirls of sunset pearl.

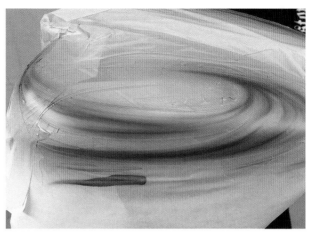

A little hot pink, and a dusting of blue intensifier, adds brightness to the swirls.

The sunset pearl is followed by multiple light passes of hot pink.

A look at the three separate, but interacting, areas before the pinstripes.

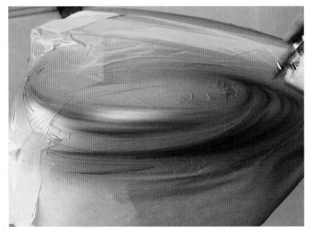

The effects are subtle, the next color to be applied is passion pearl.

After applying a quick coat of intercoat clear and allowing that to dry, Keith scrubs the tank with 800 grit wet paper "to take down the edges."

The sunset pearl is followed by hot pink (PBC 39). Using an airbrush, Keith does more swirls, overlaid on top of what was done with the sunset pearl.

Passion pearl is next (PBC 65), more swirl patterns are laid down on top of previous patterns. Back and forth, Keith adds a little more hot pink for a subtle effect, followed by some blue intensifier. Next comes a quick coat of intercoat clear.

KEITH'S COLOR THEORY

"You can put almost any color with any other if you have the right colors in between, so the pinstriping is very important. Using leaf for a pinstripe draws a lot of attention to the panel. Pinstripes are an easy way to add more punch."

Keith advises that overspray can be eliminated with some wet 1200 grit. Before doing any pinstriping the tanks are clearcoated with final clear and allowed to sit overnight. The clear is then wet sanded with 800 grit paper. "I don't use a sanding block," explains Keith, "basically, I'm just taking down the edges of the graphics."

PINSTRIPES

Keith outlines each panel with fineline tape, this tape is a guide, which is why he leaves 1/8 inch between graphic and the tape (note the nearby photos). All the pinstriping, except the leaf of course, is done with H of K striping urethane mixed with their reducer (U 00) and no catalyst. For mixing paint and reducer to the right viscosity, Keith uses a non-porous palette. The brush is a Mack brand, size 00 made from squirrel hair. "This is a bright job, says Keith, "I want bright stripes. I want a lot of contrast so I can see this job from a distance. It's important that the paint be evenly distributed throughout the brush, even if it means using your fingers to smooth out the bristles."

"I start with simple stripes first, as I did with the graphics. And mentally, when I do the easy steps first, then by the time I get to the really hard part, to me it looks like I've already got the job almost done. I also use a Mack scrolling

A piece of fineline tape run just off the edge of the graphic is used as a guide for Keith.

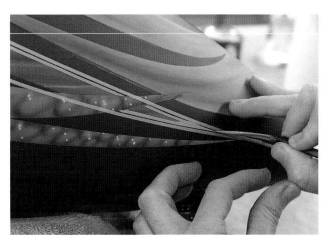

At the corners "the pinstripes can be used to elongate and exaggerate the shape."

Colors are picked on the fly.. But be careful because the urethane striping paints can't be easily wiped off if you don't like the effect.

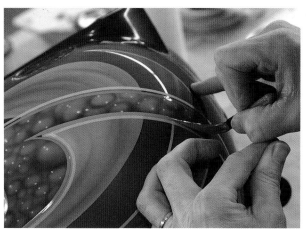

Most of the stripes are done with a conventional Mack number 00 pinstriping brush made from Squirrel hair.

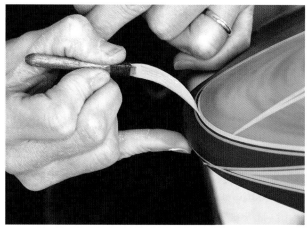

Keith mixes the size with mineral spirits to achieve the right viscosity. One-Shot gives it the color. Pinstriping brush is used for application.

For tight detail work and intersections Keith likes a small lettering brush. Brushes are cleaned in regular paint reducer from H of K, not the U 00.

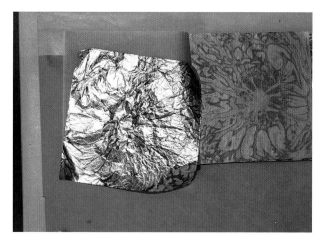

The leaf is variegated red, available from Sid Moses.

The size, or adhesive, is mixed with paint so it's easier to see.

Keith uses soft taps from the heel of his hand to fully seat the leaf onto the size.

script, it's like a small lettering brush. I use it for intersections and small areas. Peach (U 28) is the first color. I always try to use the stripes to exaggerate the shapes you already have, the stripes help to elongate the tips for example. I look at pinstriping as an extremely important part of finishing any job. The second pinstripe color is violet (U 29)."

Keith prefers Rolco sizing mixed with imitation gold paint from One-Shot, just a little to give it color. "When thinning the size I use mineral spirits," explains Keith, "as little of it as possible, just enough so the paint doesn't drag. Like I always say, 'I like to let the design talk to me.' And it seems in this case the orange section is dominant so I should use the brightest pinstripe around that area to keep it dominant, thus the use of variegated leaf."

The size is applied with a pinstripe brush. "As soon as you can touch the size and none comes off, that's when it's the right time to apply the gold," explains Keith. "I like variegated gold, it has more color and more going on. "

The main sheet of leaf is attached to the tank, large and small excess areas are torn off and moved to a new area, then tamped down again with the heel of Keith's hand. This process repeats until all the size is covered in gold leaf.

"This leaf is from Sid Moses (see sources), it's got the most color of any of the variegated products," explains Keith. "I knock off the big chunks by hand, then rub it down with a soft rag to eliminate the rest of the excess, then wipe off the gold dust with a damp rag. The size never really does dries completely."

Keith advises doing the leaf last, "because if you do it first you might have to tape over it, and you can't. And once the leaf is on, don't wash the surface with anything stronger than soap and water. I clear it immediately. As you would anything else."

The final clear Keith uses is PPG 3000, because it's affordable, works and dries fast, and offers good UV protection.

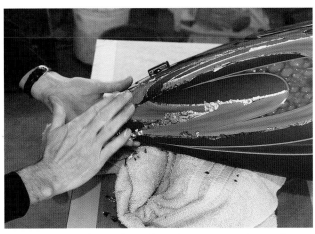

Once the leaf has adhered to the size, Keith gently pulls off the excess material, which is moved to a new area.

By rubbing the area down with a soft rag the rest of the loose leaf is pulled off.

The finished tank, minus the final clear. Compare this to the picture on page 104 and note how much impact the pinstripes have on the overall design

Chapter Eight

Andy Anderson Studio, Inc.

Part-Time Passion

Andy Anderson is more than a great painter and artist. He's also the co-owner with his wife Sherry of Anderson Studio Inc., a screen printing operation located in Downtown Nashville, Tennessee. Originally Andy and Sherry started the operation as an airbrush and custom paint studio doing work on bikes, vans and commercial illustrations for the music industry. "We added shirt printing for economical reasons," explains Andy, "and it has become a big part of ASI today. We

This candy tribal paint job has a white pearl base with candy fades. Over that a cut-black ghost flame was airbrushed before the tribal art.

still do airbrush work on bikes, along with building a few complete bikes from time to time".

Anytime Andy isn't working on the production of T-shirts for bike shops or country-western stars, he can be found in the paint booth located on the ground floor of the ASI facility. In addition to his abilities as a screen printer and painter, Andy is a pretty good photographer and writer, evidenced by the fact that all the material that follows, both the words and the images, is Andy's own.

The project seen here is what I call a rainbow tribal paint job. The customer for this job liked color and he liked hard edged Tribal Graphics. To fulfill his desire for both I started with a white pearl base, added the flames (using a cut black mixed with SG-100) and then cleared the whole thing with UC 35. Next I did a yellow candy to purple candy fade. The pieces were then recleared and wet sanded with 500 wet/dry paper to prepare them for the tribal graphics. The customer wanted his graphics bold and covering a lot of the tank and fender area so I began my layout using 1/8 and 1/16 inch tape.

The captions explain most of the job, but there are a few things that deserve special attention:

The white base for the graphics is two coats of shimrin snow white (PBC-44) sprayed over a white KS catalyzed sealer from H of K. The masking is still in place at this point. Before applying

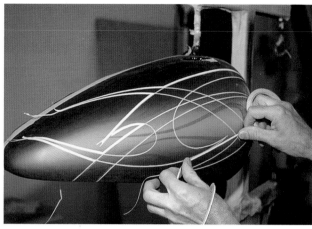

The first job is to do a layout on top of the existing paint work. I use 1/8th and 1/16th inch tape for this.

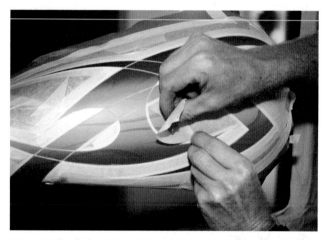

Once I had the layout I liked, I began to tape off the design and prepare the graphics for the base color. You can use 2 inch tape or vinyl transfer paper.

…we do this in order to spray down a solid uninterrupted white pearl base.

Once the design was masked I had to cut the existing layout fineline tape out of the inside of my design…

The final layout, all that's left is to wipe it down with wax and grease remover to get rid of any tape residue. I also use a tack rag before I spray.

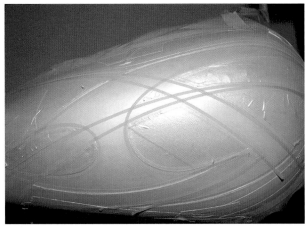

By taping it out this way it allows the base white to remain when the tape is pulled giving a nice crisp edge to the bevel.

The white is 2 light coats of snow white (PBC-44) sprayed over H of K KS white sealer, over thinned slightly. Then 2-3 coats of SG 100 intercoat clear and sand with 800. You could also use Scotch-Brite.

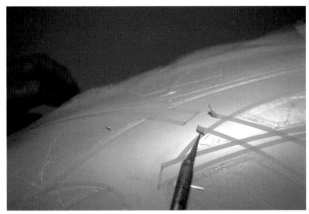

At this point I have to determine which parts of the design go over and which go under.

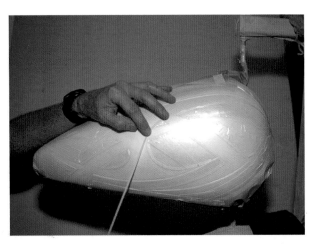

This is where I begin masking off the beveled edges of the Tribal Graphics.

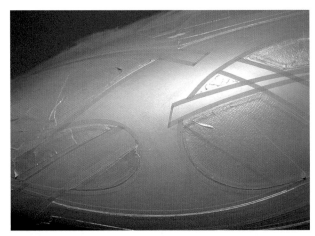

Deciding which goes over or under requires a lot of thought...

the actual graphics, I cleared the white with H of K intercoat clear and then sand with 800 grit. Sanding with 800 grit gets rid of dust nibs. And after scuffing the graphics can sit for as long as necessary and you still get good adhesion of the topcoats.

BEVELED EDGES

This is where I begin masking off the beveled edges of the tribal graphics. It's very crucial that these edges are even and consistent throughout the design. This keeps a sense of balance and uniformity to your layout. It is visually OK to use a 1/8 inch edge on one of the graphics and then have a spear that comes through that design with only a 1/16th edge around it. I personally don't like to mix different widths on my edges because I like the balance and continuity that one size gives

The white pearl gives a good base for the edge bevel. When doing tape cross-overs, be careful to get the over and unders rights. I also go over all the outer edges of my masking so I don't have gaps between the edge tape and the background tape that might accidentally get sprayed and leave an unwanted color on my beveled edge (check the photo on the bottom of this page).

I'm always mixing paint to get just the right color. The blue is actually a candy blue with a little purple (KK 10) and black. The colors I use are the H of K kandy koncentrates mixed with SG 100. I start with oriental blue (KK 04).

The darker blues that precede the lightest blue, as seen in the sequence on page 111 are the same light blue with more oriental blue purple and black, with an emphasis on the purple and black to darken it.

Once I have the darker blue over my lighter blue (middle photo) I come in at the edge and airbrush in a very cut black to darken the fade even more. Be careful, it doesn't take much to kill your candy blends.

You really want to control your blends to show the white pearl base on the opposite side of the face to represent a highlight. White pearl is a very important element of this type of design. When allowed to come through the design in key areas it provides depth and dimension which helps with the 3-D effect.

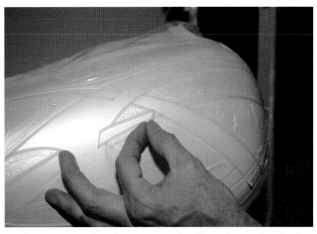

…be sure to take the time to think it through - before you start cutting and spraying.

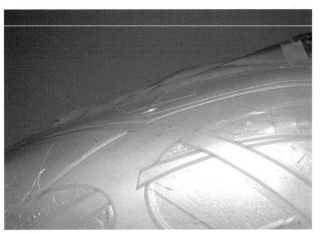

This is the complete design on the tank with the over and unders trimmed out. The fineline tape masks out the bevels on the edges of the spears.

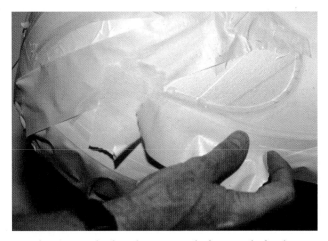

At this point the bevels are taped, first with fineline then with 1/4 inch. Now I'm masking prior to shooting the face of the tribal design.

Q&A: Andy Anderson

How did you get started with painting and air-brush work?

In the mid to late 1960s I got caught up in what was going on, everything from mini bikes to motorcycles. I became inspired by the stuff I saw in the magazines. During high school I worked with my friend Clyde McCullough at his Dad's dealership. We assembled little Yamahas, but the dealership handled Harleys too and I picked up a basket-Panhead.

About the same time I started experimenting with paint. I used to cut open spray cans to get the metal-flake color I wanted and then spray the paint through my airbrush. Then I'd borrow a friend's compressor to do the clearcoat. Up to that point I was totally self taught, I just learned from doing and asking other guys how they did it. In 1971 I went to work full time as the painter for C&S Custom Cycles. We had a knucklehead that won the Rat's Hole show. It was a pretty impressive bike for the time with a molded Sporty tank, a nineteen-over springer fork, electric start and wild paint.

Some people with a successful screen-printing business would be content with that - but Andy needs motorcycle projects like the rest of us need air.

Do you have any formal art training?

Yes I do. Later I took four years of advertising art and illustration. I learned good color theory and anatomy. This was all old school. I learned how to mix colors and use oils. When I graduated I thought I'd go to an ad agency and make good money, but I found out I was making more doing custom paint. So I opened Anderson Studios and ended up doing covers for record companies. The money was good, but again, that wasn't what I really enjoyed. For a while I didn't do painting because our new building didn't have a booth anymore and the custom bike thing kind of fell off, too. That's when we started doing T-shirts. We did shirts for acts like Kenny Rogers and Marty Robins, and the local Harley shop.

What do you like to use for paint?

I use lots of H of K and PPG, I don't mix the systems though. I might do work with H of K materials, then cover that with a H of K clear, and then go over the top with PPG materials (after sanding).

What do you have for airbrushes?

I have an old workhorse Paache VL, but I also have a bunch of Iwatas, the Eclipse and the microns. I like the Iwata line a lot.

Do you have any tips for using automotive paint in airbrush?

I over-reduce it and use slower reducer so it keeps the paint from drying on the tip which helps to keep it flowing. You need to keep the paint well strained and mixed. I've used everything from base coats to striping enamels, even metal flakes. Sometimes I use gravity-feed touch up guns in place of an airbrush.

Where do you get your ideas?

I watch and read everything from bike magazines to art magazines. In years past a lot of my color work came from color combinations I saw in butterflies and tropical fish. If you sit down and look at the creatures that are out there, there's a little fish with a beautiful fuschia to orange fade, the colors are just incredible. I look at the masters and older illustrations. And I try an accommodate what the customer wants. The initial sketches have my influence, but I still have to keep the customer happy.

SHADING AND HIGHLIGHTS

Starting at the top of page 115, the top left photo shows me working on the top edge where a spear is going over and through another design. In order to create the depth necessary to give this a 3-D look the airbrush shading on the edges is crucial especially where the shadow of a spear coming through needs to be. The upper edge bevel behind the protruding spear is taped off in order to darken, or shade, that area and give it depth. I use the previous dark blue with a little more black to gray the color a bit more. This shadow should not be very dark, but basically subtle so as to make a difference in the lightest areas of the upper bevels and those in shadow. Use discretion here.

Again, as mentioned when doing the other bevel edges (left middle photo), tape it out to allow the base white of the bevel to be airbrushed. Airbrush your cut dark blue along the upper edge of the lower loop bevel. Allow white to show at the bottom. Bottom left shows the design unmasked with most of the airbrush shading complete. The only other shading to be done is the detail shading where the spear comes through the background tribal (bottom right, page 115). I taped off an angular shadow to be sprayed to the left of the protruding spear. This is airbrushed from a dark blue toward the inside going lighter to the bevel itself.

Note, I added shadows coming off all protruding spears to add dimensional form. It's very critical that you pay attention to your light source when doing highlights and shadows. You are ready to clear at this point.

I usually put on four to five coats of UC 35 clear and wet sand with 500. I might clear again to bury the artwork. Final clears are allowed to dry overnight. Then I sand with 1000, 1500, 2000 and 3000, if necessary, to get a slick surface to buff. I use 3-M extra-cut compound and a foam pad, followed by regular compound and a foam pad and finally the 3-M Finesse final buff with a waffle-style foam pad. I don't recommend any waxing for at least 60 days to allow the paint to fully cure.

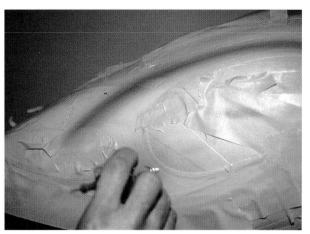

I begin my airbrush work using a mixed candy color. I started with candy blue mixed in SG-100, and tinted it with a touch of purple and black.

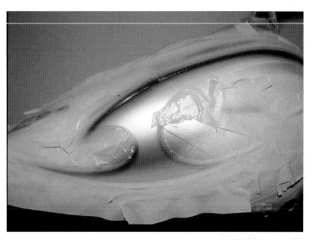

I begin to darken the blue with a separate color basically using the same blue candy, purple, and black with a bit more purple and black.

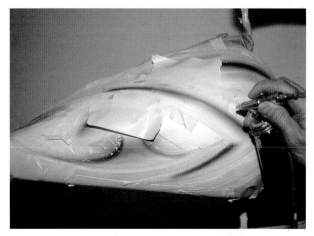

Here I'm adding black to the upper edge.

113

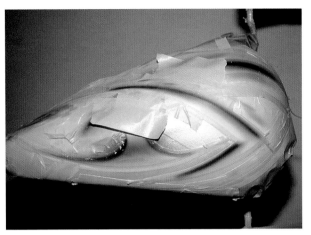

The cut black used close to the edge enhances the contrast.

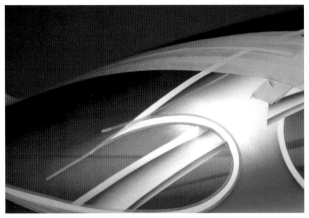

Tape outline shows portion of a spear that needs shading in shadows of curve to give it depth. Upper part of job shows an area taped out to spray another shadow along the bottom edge of another spear.

This is a better close up of the airbrush fade. Note that the bottom edge of the design still allows the white pearl base to show.

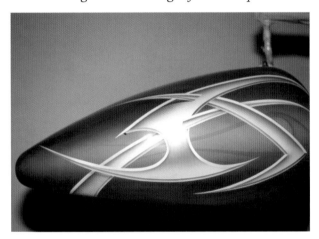

This picture shows bottom edge of tribal art with it's subtle shadows. The top edge is still solid white pearl and needs a little airbrushing to give it form.

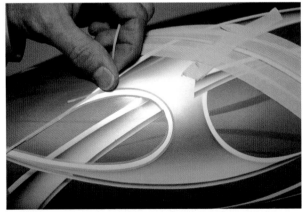

After most of the interior airbrushing, I unmask to reveal the work. Then I come back in and retape some outside bevels and airbrushed shadows, or fades, where needed. I do this using the 1/16 inch tape to outline my design for airbrushing.

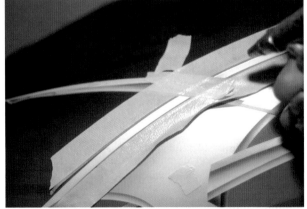

The top edge taped and ready to airbrush. I begin near the overlaps to give a sense of depth to the graphic spears where they go over each other.

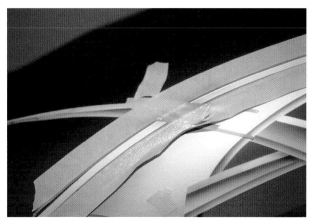

This photo shows the edges of the overlap slightly shaded, with a darker grayed blue used to make the shadows.

Note the additional shadows where the tribal spears come through...

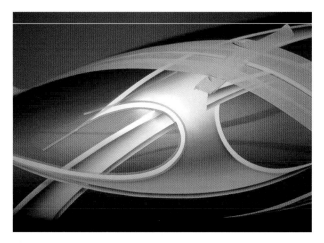

The overlaps are taped to shadow the outside bottom edge of the bevels.

...where the spears protrude I taped out a tapered shadow to really show how the spear rises up above the background.

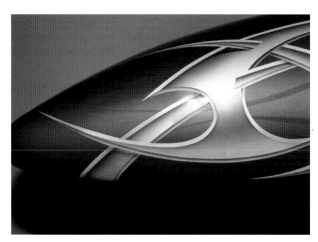

All the tribal graphics and beveled edges unmasked and edges finished airbrushing.

Close up shows the depth that this technique gives the artwork.

Chapter Nine

Leah Gall

A Sexy Pinup

Hidden away in an old restored barn well north of Minneapolis is Finishline Inc., the small paint and graphics operation of the husband and wife team of Leah and Brian Gall. While Brian does graphics, as well as all the basecoats and clear

in their downdraft booth, Leah toils away in her own area, airbrushing everything imaginable on to mostly motorcycle sheet metal.

In this particular case the customer and bike owner asked that her likeness be airbrushed onto

Wilde Thing is a Chopper decorated with images of the owner, Yvette Wilde. The main image is a good example of just how much work it is to airbrush a realistic human figure.

the old-skool tank of her new Klock Werks chopper. Working from photos, Leah starts the job by sketching out Yvette in various poses, using photographs for reference, to determine which looks best and which best fits the shape of the tank. As Leah explains, "I do a lot of just drawing and tracing of photographs. In a situation like this I like to draw something out a couple of times so I really know the subject."

Once she has a good sketch Leah makes a mask for the outside of the design, explaining, "some people do this on the tank, but I don't like to work on the tank if I don't have to." The masking material is MACtac, a low-tack sign painter's material that Leah likes because it cuts nice and it's economical.

CUT IT CLOSE

After trimming the mask and covering it with a piece of transfer material, Leah sticks it onto the flat face of the tank, tapes off the areas surrounding the mask and sprays the tank with two coats of a very light skin tone color that really functions as a sealer for the blue, and a basecoat for all the painting to follow.

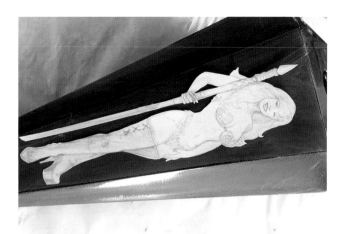

Early on, Leah positions the sketch on the tank to see how it fits.

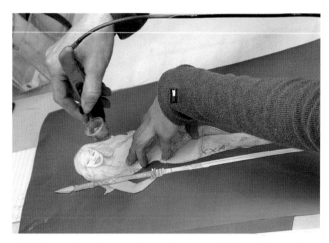

A light mist of paint is used to mark the outline of the sketch on a piece of masking material...

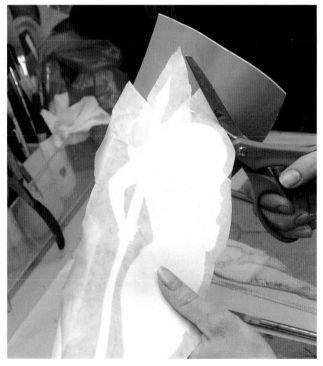

With the transfer paper in place, the main mask is trimmed before Leah puts it on the tank.

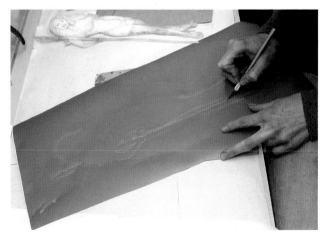

...which is cut out before it is applied to the tank.

117

Here the transfer material is peeled off, leaving the basic mask in place.

Before starting on the job Leah mixes up various lighter and darker versions of the skin tone color.

Now the rest of the tank can be masked off.

The mask for the boots is cut out one small section at a time...

Two coats of basic flesh-tone paint are applied first.

...following outlines drawn in with a ball-point pen.

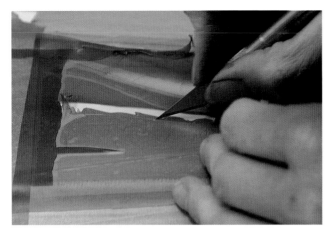

1) The actual cutting is done in multiple steps...

2)...each individual piece of mask is pulled off and saved for back masking later.

The beginning skin tone color is mixed from white, yellow and a little darker yellow with just a little orange tint. "I go back and forth until I like what I see and it just looks right," explains Leah. "In this case I added just a tiny bit of blue violet. I always try it on a bit of paper to see if I like the color."

"If it's not warm enough the first time, I add a little white and some red. Based on that basic color I also mix a variety of flesh tones, some lighter and some darker, including a designated shadow tone and a lighter rosy skin tone for highlight areas." The paint colors are mixed using clear pearl base with white, yellow, dark yellow, orange and blue-violet" (all from the Xotic line of tint-pastes).

3) Here you can see how an area that will be a medium gray is pulled out, leaving what will be a lighter reflective section in place.

PAINTING STARTS

The two coats of skin-tone paint Leah puts down act as the base color for all the painting to follow, and also ensures that the candy basepaint that's already on the tank can't bleed through and affect the color of the airbrush work.

THESE BOOTS ARE MADE FOR POSING

Using the original sketch as a guide for registration, Leah puts down another layer of masking material that covers the legs and feet. This will become the stencil for the long, black patent leather boots.

After trimming the new mask Leah marks the outline and details of the boots right on the mask

4) Thinned out black is used to paint this area.

119

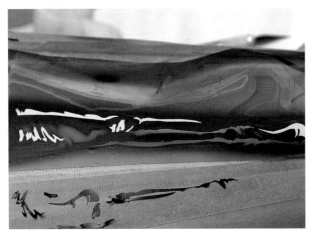

Here you can see the left boot done and unmasked.

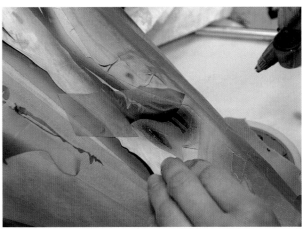

Next the sole and heel are painted a medium black with the highlights masked off.

A separate mask is used for the lower boot.

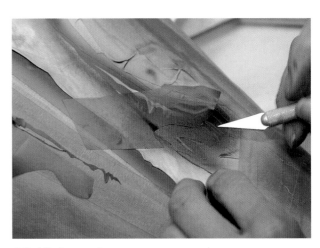

Highlight masks are now removed...

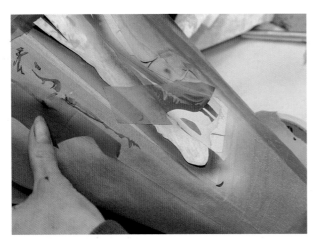

Most of the heel and sole are cut away from the rest of the mask. Note how the "highlights" are left in place.

...and those areas are painted lightly with a thinned black, one highlight area is left masked so the highlight will be white.

In the case of the reflection that runs the length of the boot, part of it is left "white" and part is shaded gray.

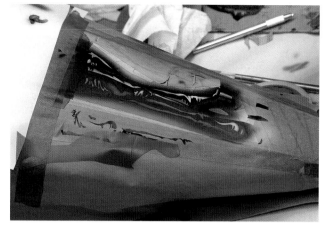

Research for a picture can take a lot of time because you're looking for references of all the details.

This tracing is the first step in the creation of a new sheer lingerie outfit.

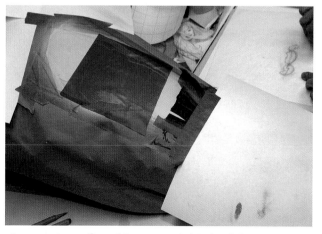

A new piece of masking material is laid down over the main part of the body.

with a ball-point pen, using catalog pictures as a guide. Cutting out the mask or stencil is actually a multi-step process. Because the boots aren't just "black" Leah needs to cut out each shade of black individually. In some cases an area is cut out but the central area containing a bright highlight is left in place. In this way she can spray the just-uncovered-area with light transparent black, and then pull the mask, creating an area that's light black with a white reflection in the very center. In this patient and time-consuming way Leah creates a very bright and believable pair of high-heeled boots.

THE BODY BEAUTIFUL

Before Leah can start on the body the customer calls and asks that the warrior uniform be swapped for a lingerie. Which means the spear must morph into a brass pole. To start the process she first traces important features of the sketch onto a piece of tracing paper. Next, the back side of the tracing paper is coated with chalk to make it a image transfer sheet. Now the tracing paper can be placed over the tank, over the new piece of masking material placed (using the original sketch only as an aid in registration) so features can be

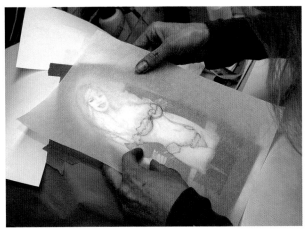

The original sketch is used to help register the new tracing.

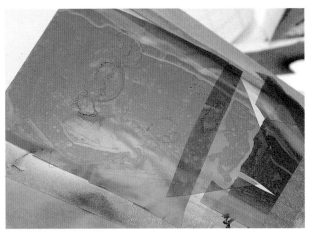

MACtac masking material ready to cut.

Once the position of the tracing is determined the sketch can be pulled out of the sandwich. The back of this tracing paper is coated with chalk.

The mask is cut leaving only the barest parts of the bikini in place. I have a light color under the mask which will become part of the feathery texture.

By going over the tracing with a ball-point pen (or any stylus) the outline is transferred to the masking material underneath.

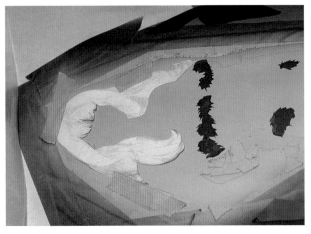

With the hair stencil set in place loosely, Leah sprays on the overly warm base for the skin color.

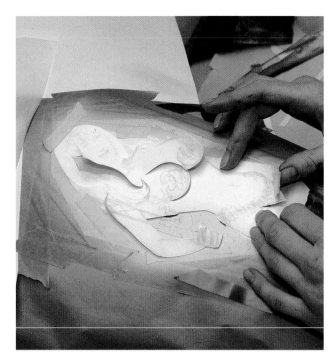

A mask like this with cutouts or windows makes it easy to peel back one area at a time and apply paint with no worries about overspray.

transferred to the mask. When she's all done, the only parts of the masking material left on the tank are the "fluffy" parts of the lingerie.

MORE STENCILS

Before proceeding Leah makes three new masks or stencils. One represents the hair, so the upper body and face can be painted in without getting overspray into the areas that will become long blonde locks. The other two are body masks, "because you can't do all the cutting on one stencil," explains Leah, "they get beat up as you work. I scan my sketch into the computer and print out multiple copies so I can make more than one stencil."

The next step is to apply a skin-tone basecoat over the whole body area. Then with a lighter color in the airbrush Leah starts to outline the breasts and the left arm, followed by some highlights on various body parts.

Switching to a slightly darker color, Leah begins to sculpt the various details that make up the body, explaining as she does, "For this I'm using a mixture of basic skin tone color combined

Following the application of a lighter color the skin tone is looking more like skin tone.

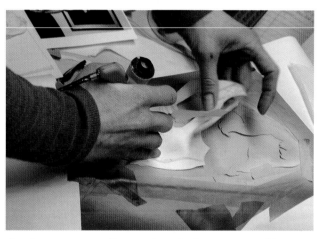

Leah starts to outline various body parts, working first with light paint and a mask...

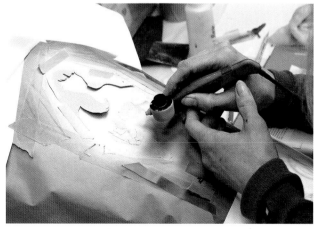

...then freehand with a slightly darker color.

Q&A: Leah Gall

Leah, let's start with your background and training?

I don't have any formal training, I just picked it up. I've been painting since I was a kid. For six years I worked at the mall, airbrushing. People would ask me to do almost anything. That's where I had to learn how to draw all these things they would ask for, from cars to football players. And they would want me to put them on almost anything. license plates, helmets, T-shirts, jackets. That was good experience. Eventually I started going to Daytona, in fact one year I worked for Big Daddy Rat. We did a lot of helmets and jackets and that kind of thing.

Where did you learn how to use and mix color?

Like I said, I painted when I was little. My dad had a little body shop, I mixed paint for him. A few years ago I took a class from Dru Blair and that helped, but I think I'm just good at color and mixing color.

How much do you use the computer?

I sketch a lot but then the computer is useful to flip-flop an image, or size an image up or down to better fit the panel.

What kind of airbrush do you like?

I've used Aztek airbrushes for years, because it's easy to adjust the airflow. They are dual action like the others, but I call them triple-action because you can adjust the air pressure by how hard you push down on the trigger.

And it's easy to change the tips. The tips come in different sizes, all enclosed as an assembly with the tip and needle. They work great, they are a great value.

What do you like for paint?

We use X-otic paint. I like it because it's easy to make up my own colors - I'm an artist and I love color and their system makes it so easy to make my own colors. You can start with a neutral base or a pearl base and then add toners. And you don't need much paint.

There are color pastes too. You can mix unusual colors, translucent colors, makeup your own pinstripe color, it's great.

Some artists have trouble with the human form, tell us your approach.

I make pencil sketches first, and more than one pose. Usually I chose the second or third sketch. I like to paint voluptuous figures, daVinciesque bodies with rich skin tones. I like to idealize the form, I don't paint exactly what I see.

Self taught, Leah is comfortable painting graphics, murals or the human form onto mostly motorcycle sheet metal. Like a number of airbrush artists, Leah often uses a fine brush to add detail to her airbrush designs.

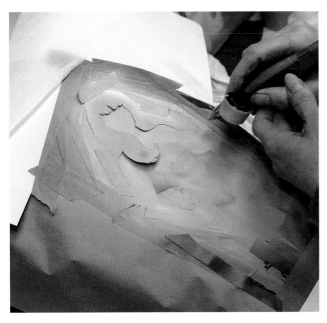

...that define muscles and body contours. The paint hue is based on skin tone color with a little shadow color and a small amount of purple.

The body develops slowly, here a darker color is used to create shadows...

with a small amount of the shadow color and a little purple to give the skin a tan look." The process of painting with lighter and darker tones continues until recognizable body parts emerge from the masked area.

THE MOST IMPORTANT STENCIL

Based on the separate facial sketch Leah did earlier, she now cuts a very detailed facial mask. With slightly darker paint in the airbrush she is able to create the basic outline of the face including the eyes, eyebrows, nose and mouth. "I will have to touch this up freehand later," explains Leah, "using the same color paint." Next is the neck, "it's a tricky area." For much of the neck area Leah uses a mask, either the body mask made earlier or small masks used to confine the paint to one area or create a clean well-defined line like that along the collar bone.

DETAILS FOR THE UPPER BODY AND FACE

"As I work through this area," explains Leah, "I am defining form and muscle. I keep darkening the work shade by shade until I have reached the desired appearance."

Now a series of highlights are added over the dark color, "it's going to look a little funny for a while," warns Leah. Highlights are added to the

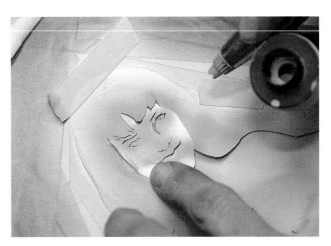

A carefully constructed mask, and darker skin-tone paint, is used to begin crafting the face.

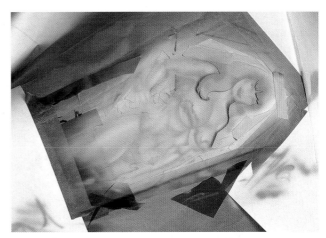

A progress shot shows the figure's development.

125

With the hair mask in place Leah adds highlights to the upper body...

After adding a few highlights the painting still looks a little too dark at this stage.

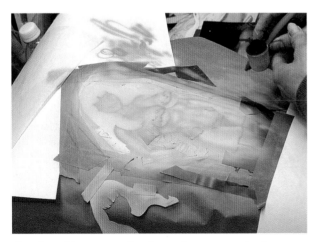

...and the face using skin-tone mixed with a little white, and even less orange.

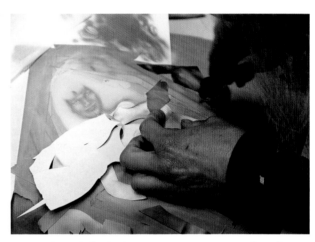

A mask and dark skin-tone paint are used to further detail the body with additional shadows.

Darker skin tone paint is used to create shadows and to tint the whole body darker.

Though still a little dark, this progress shot shows a rather well developed body.

126

face and neck, (see the photos on the facing page) and body parts like the ribs and tops of thighs. The color is white with a touch of orange added to the original skin tone mix. "If you add just white to something to lighten it can go toward the blue end of the spectrum," explains Leah, "so I included the orange in the mix. I have to thank Dru Blair for that tip."

Painting a body like this is definitely a case of subtle changes. Unlike a graphic that moves in a pretty linear fashion from the start to the finish, the face and body being painted here move in a long series of very subtle steps from off-white to a hundred shades of "skin tone." When Leah has the body pretty well developed she wipes the work off with a tack rag and applies a coat of intercoat clear to protect the work done so far.

LINGERIE AND HAIR

To dress our blonde in a sheer outfit Leah uses a series of masks and some transparent gray paint, explaining as she does, "I'm going to start light and go darker."

Starting on the hair, Leah uses the same gray with a tiny bit of flesh tone color added. Next she does a darker blonde color, created with red shadow tones, with a drop of yellow and mix with thinned-down grey-black.

1) With the body pretty far along, it's time to start on the hair. "You could spend a whole day on her hair."

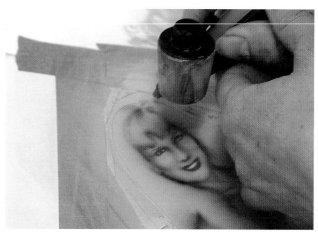

2) Coloring the hair starts with a light application (so light it's hard to see) of skin-tone paint with a little black.

3) The darker blonde color is applied first to the edges and a few deep shadows.

4) The darker blonde color is a reddish-yellow mix, combined with thinned-down-black.

127

A mask is used for much of this work so the blonde color doesn't affect the skin tones nearby.

Again, a mask is used as more of the darker blonde mix is applied.

Much of the hair texture is created by painting with quick passes of the airbrush.

Leah takes the hair a little too dark...

Pass by pass, the hair with all it's light and dark areas develops.

...seen easily in this progress shot. "But I will come back later and go over it with a lighter color."

At this point Leah begins more development of hair and shadows. This work, done in a series of short quick passes with the airbrush, leaves the impression that the hair is made up of individual strands.

ADD A MASK

For much of the work on the hair, Leah uses a mask to limit the effect. Like the rest of this work, patience is required to create believable hair with the right color and texture. "You could spend a whole day on the hair," says Leah. "It might be over-darkened now but I will come back and go over it later with a lighter color." To protect the work done so far Leah puts intercoat clear over the whole thing.

CHEEKBONES

Now I'm going to to make the face a little bit more her own," explains Leah "I want to give her more prominent cheek bones, with skin shadow colors. And I use a little peach color to add a little blush to her face."

The evolution of the face continues as Leah mixes a light flesh tone and yellow together to make a yellow/gold mix to add more color and highlights to the hair.

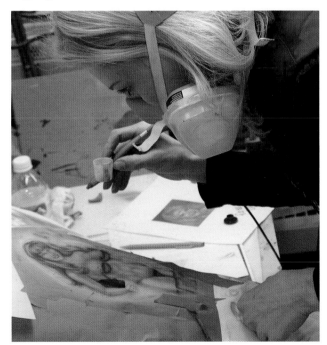

After finishing the hair it's time to add more facial details.

A rosy tint is used to create pleasant highlights on the nose and cheeks.

The endless subtle changes include lighter colors added to the hair.

The facial stencil created earlier is used now to warm up her lips.

129

This is the palette of colors Leah will need to do the fine brush work needed to finish the facial details.

Black with a dark tan color is used for eyeliner. "Part of what I'm trying to do is match the style of her makeup."

Yvette's photo is used often for reference.

A darker skin tone is used to detail part of the face, including the nose. "My brushes get smaller over time as I pick out the bad bristles"

Light blue paint, a fine paint brush, and a steady hand are used to give our blonde her sexy blue eyes.

Leah spots in little sparkles on the bikini by hand.

Back and forth, after adding the bright color to the hair Leah goes back to very light applications of the original hair color to mellow the highlights. Next, she works on the highlights, bringing them up with a fairly light tone. Some of these highlights on the thighs, stomach, neck and cheeks are a little hard to see.

BRUSH WORK, THEN THE AIRBRUSH

"When I have to do the details like on the face, it's very handy to use a brush," explains Leah. A little light blue is used for the eyes, these details really bring the face to life.

It's time now to take off the furry masks on the bikini, and add some color to that part of her outfit. Next comes the pole, which starts with more masking.

After taping, the pole is done in multiple steps using gold basecoat paint, faded at the ends, with pearl base tinted with gold for the actual color. Shadows are done with brown-gold. Highlights are created in multiple steps starting with gold pearl mixed with gold, and then white pearl, sprayed with a piece of tape in place to make a highlight line with a light application of white pearl.

Though a series of pinstripes will be added later, the main figure is essentially finished, requiring only a few details and a good clearcoat.

After removing the masks, the fluffy material is given shape with light applications of thinned black.

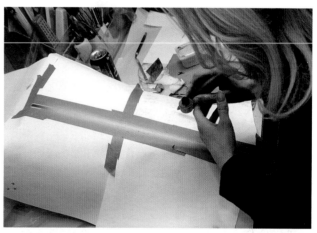

Even something as simple as a pole requires multiple taping sessions and application of many "brass" colors.

Note all the little things, like the subtle shadow of the pole on her arm. And the details to the fingers and finger nails, done by hand.

Parts of the bikini were painted by hand, using off-white paint with a little pearl flake added to the mix.

The image is finished, though pinstripes and a few additional details are still to come.

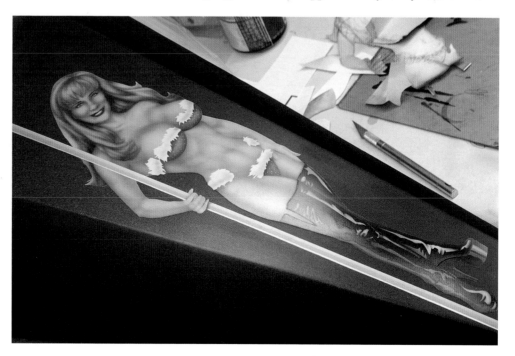

Chapter Ten

Chris Cruz

A Graphic from the King of Murals

Chris Cruz from Deland, Florida might be called "master of the mural." Though he is best known for murals and wildlife scenes often painted on motorcycles, he does a full range of projects, everything from graphics to flames. The project seen here is one of Chris' graphic jobs, done on a "32 Ford" body that will eventually end up on a Boss Hoss trike belonging to Daytona Boss Hoss.

When the project starts the body is already basecoated and covered with a special clear. "We

At Chris Cruz Artistry the projects range from motorcycles to cars and even Boss Hoss trikes. In most cases Chris and crew do the complete job, from basecoat to clear.

use a special mix of clears," explains Chris: "PPG DCA 468 clear lacquer, (up to 20 %) mixed with SG100, reduced 150 to 200% with PPG DTL 105 reducer, (this is a lacquer reducer). You don't have to sand it in between, you can leave the surface for up to several weeks and you don't have to sand the clear before coming in with more base paint. We use this because straight SG 100 is too porous, the mix of lacquer clear and SG is less porous, it's easy to wipe off a mistake or work you don't like."

Chris uses china marker to mark the body, explaining as he does, "I like to sketch right on the body, if it's simple I just go right to the object I'm painting without doing a sketch first." In this case the customer did give Chris a photo of a graphic he likes, so the end design will be Chris' interpretation of that graphic.

"I use green fineline tape," explains Chris. "The blue stuff from 3M wants to roll up when it's been on the vehicle for awhile. This is 1/8th but when I have tighter corners to lay out I go with 1/16th inch."

During the layout on the main body, not the decklid, Chris spends considerable time looking first at one side, and then the other, to ensure the taped design is positioned the same from one side to the other. The green fineline tape can be picked up and put back down and still maintain good adhesion.

"Now I'm starting to see the whole thing in my head," says Chris. "Where the colors go and which part of the design goes over or under the other."

"For trimming the tape I use a razor blade for big areas and a Xacto knife for more intricate areas. The trick is to avoid cutting too deep. On the decklid I'm going to do the layout in stages as I paint. On the upper part of the body I'm going to do the layout all at once at the beginning, before doing any paint. It's interesting to try different methods sometimes to see which is more efficient."

START PAINTING

In order to better follow this fairly complex project, we've focused on the trunklid. Chris starts by explaining the difference in graphics and

Chris draws the design right on the surface, which is clearcoated with his special clear:

Next comes fineline tape....

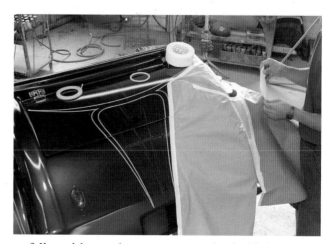

...followed by masking paper. On the decklid Chris is masking out one section at a time instead of all at once.

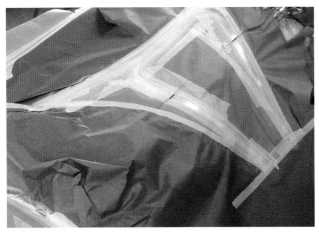

1) Basecoat white with a little yellow is the first color, the yellow will help tint this closer to the final topcoat color.

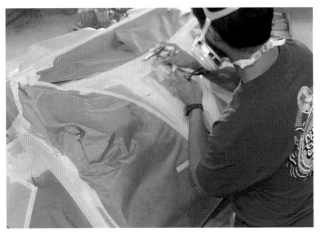

2) Next comes the special-mix yellow...

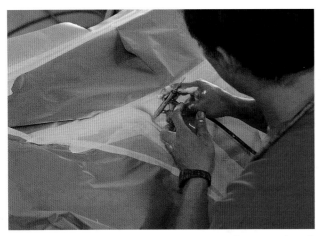

4) The mini-flames start as almost random streaks of orange.

murals. "For murals I use mostly solid basecoat colors, for graphics like this I often use candies or pearls."

Chris starts with what he calls pre-basecoat white. This "white" has a little yellow mixed in so it will match the yellow (the actual topcoat color) better. Now comes the real color for this section, bright yellow. This color is one of Chris' special mixes, a combination of chrome yellow and lime yellow. Chris applies two coats of the mix.

Bright orange is next, used to create what Chris calls "flame streaks" on top of the yellow. These are actually little mini flames, and they're done so quick it's hard to follow the sequence with the camera (my attempt to document their creation can be seen on the facing page). Chris does an outline on one side of a "flame lick," then another on the other side then comes back and quickly fills the area between the outlines with a soft mist of orange. It happens so fast it looks like he's just doing a series of random streaks until you stop and examine the effect.

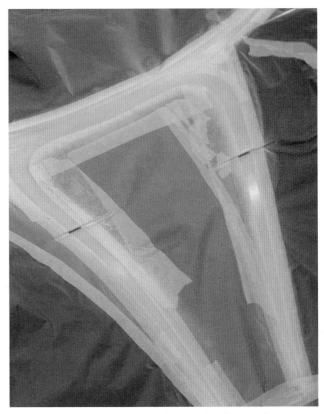

3) ...applied in two coats for good color and coverage.

The sequence on this page shows the development of the mini-flames.

Chris pulls the airbrush away occasionally and fills in the area between two strong outlines of orange.

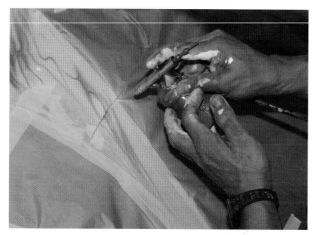

Which develop so fast they just seem to "happen."

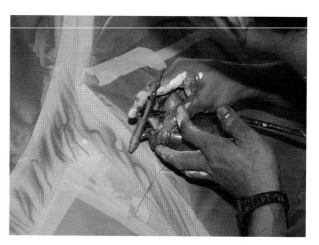

More close work to create a fine line.

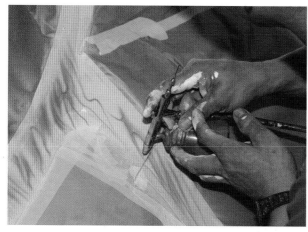

The airbrush is held close for most of the work, the movements are very fast and fluid.

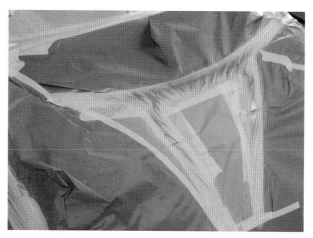

The finished work looks like a ring of fire laid across the trunklid.

All the tape masking off the yellow spear is pulled...

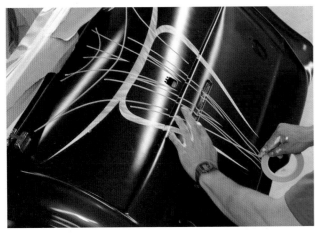

...before Chris can start on the second layout. Both layouts follow the outlines sketched onto the body earlier.

Dark grey is a base for the red...

When the little mini-flames are finished Chris shoots a clearcoat, using his special mix again.

UN-TAPE - RE-TAPE

As was described earlier, the decklid is going to be taped off one section at a time. Which means Chris pulls the tape, examines his work, and then tapes out the new area (note the photos on this page).

The first color to be applied is a dark grey used in the center of the new masked off area as a base and to block out areas where the yellow shows. This is the area that will be painted red. Chris describe this as, "a very opaque color that covers well."

The second base color to be applied is off-white, which is the base for the areas that will be painted orange. Everyone has their own style. In the case of Chris Cruz, the work goes fast. Once the taping is done the painting progresses very quickly. (Note: The red and orange are not the finish colors.)

Once the grey and off-white are dry Chris comes in with red for the center and orange for the outer areas, (H of K euro red and bright orange). Next, Chris uses the red to create a red-to-orange fade on the edges of the orange areas.

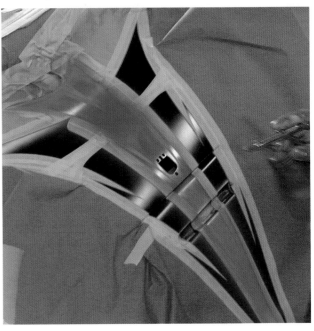

...chosen partly because it covers the yellow easily.

Q&A Chris Cruz

How did you get started and do you have any formal art training?

I remember in 3rd grade, the teacher asked us to draw a tree. So I drew a tree and put individual leaves on each branch. The other kids were drawing lollipop trees. Later, I joined poster contests and used the airbrush as my main tool. In high school I had a really good art teacher who taught me everything from commercial art and design to fine arts. I followed him after high school, taking his classes in community college. Through him, I was able to get better with my skills, especially my oil portraits on canvas.

How did the interest in custom painting on vehicles develop?

My dad had a motorcycle shop in Scottsville, Virginia. Our family vacation meant going to Daytona during Bike Week, so as a kid I saw airbrushing on T-shirts and pinstriping on bikes and cars. I just really took interest in that. I practiced airbrushing, pin striping, and hand-lettering everything from shirts to vehicles and signs.

You seem to be best known for murals. How did that come to pass? And how are murals different from graphics? Can you touch on your techniques?

My knack for airbrushed murals stems from my background in fine art. I learned how to airbrush in high detail and how to work with colors to achieve depth. The background in fine art also helped me lean more toward creating murals that looked realistic as a portrait would. I started out doing fantasy murals on vans back in the late 80's. At about the same time we moved to Florida and I started doing murals and pinstriping mostly for the Honda Gold Wing riders. Murals are different from graphics in that, for me, murals are more illustrations of natural and realistic subjects and backgrounds. Graphics are designs that can be abstract, that are more hard-edged, that do not show people, animals, or scenery.

In terms of technique, in my murals I generally work from background to foreground. In the background I generally use duller and cooler colors with less detail to create distance. As I work into the foreground, I may paint with more vivid colors and increase the detail in the artwork. Usually in the

foreground, or the main subject, I will use the brightest and most contrasting colors, painting with highest detail. I paint with more opaque colors. I start off painting a mid-tone, and then add shadows, and later on, highlights. I may also use some transparent colors to work with the shadows and highlights. And some transparent colors to achieve a finer and more delicate blend in certain cases.

What do you like for paint?

I use mostly base coats with some lacquers, clear-coating the final artwork with urethane clears. My choice of paints are H of K, PPG, and Restorer's Choice for clear coats. We always shoot an adhesion promoter on top of our artwork prior to the clear, since we exceed the re-coat window. Sherwin-Williams S-64 is my favorite.

Where do you get your ideas?

My ideas vary, depending on what the client wants. The theme, the subject, all determine a starting point. In my mind there is a reference file that has grown through the years. I also keep a large reference file of books, photos and clippings. The books are mostly illustrative and vary in subjects that include nature and wildlife, art illustration, realistic and fantasy, historical, cultural, pretty much every subject. Some of my favorite artists are Sorayama, Vargas, Boris Vallejo, Frazetta, Bev Doolittle, Judy Larsen, Frank McCarthy, Dru Blair, and Bateman.

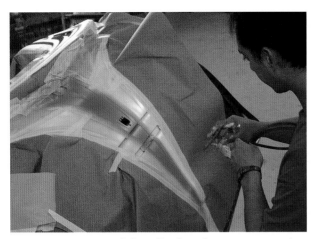

Again, two coats of the off-white base assure good coverage.

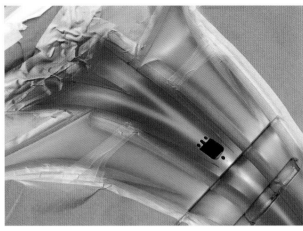

Here you can see how Chris used the red to outline and brighten the orange. Highlight in the center is done in hot pink pearl.

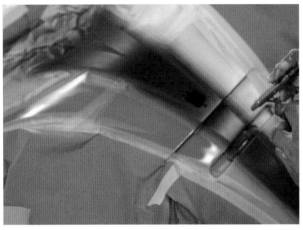

The red goes on first, followed by orange. These two colors are only the starting point.

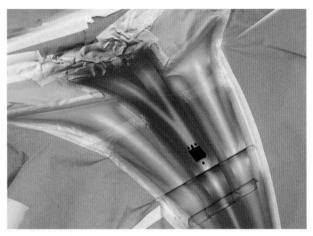

Yellow is chosen as the highlight color for the orange.

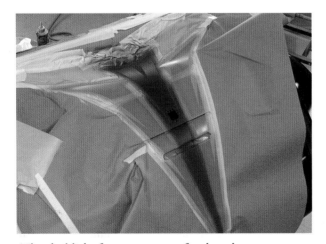

The decklid after two coats of red and orange.

A mist of magenta tints the center V and highlight.

To brighten the dark central red V, Chris applies a V-shaped spear of hot pink pearl (PBC 39). And to create a similar highlight on the orange area a streak of yellow is added to each orange area. Before declaring this step finished and masking off the area a mist of magenta is used to tint the red and hot pink.

Now the central V is masked off and a mist of orange pearl is used to richen the orange on the outside of the design.

Chris makes the highlights on the decklid hotter by adding a little more yellow on the orange areas and white on the red area.

At this point the basic design is finished, at least on the decklid. To protect the work Chris applies a clearcoat, then pulls the tape.

PINSTRIPE

"Before starting on the pinstriping," explains Chris, "I have to scuff the clearcoat with 800-grit paper. What's next are the the actual pinstripes.

The paint is pinstripe urethane from H of K, and the first color is process blue. When it comes to picking the color for the pinstripes I just go by my gut."

Like most experienced pinstripers, Chris does

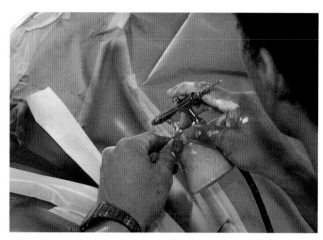

After tinting the orange with orange pearl, a little more yellow is added to the highlights.

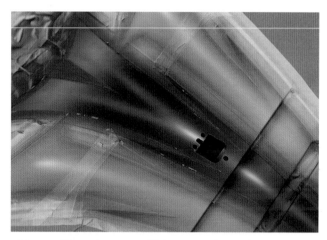

After pulling the tape off the central V, Chris uses white to create highlights.

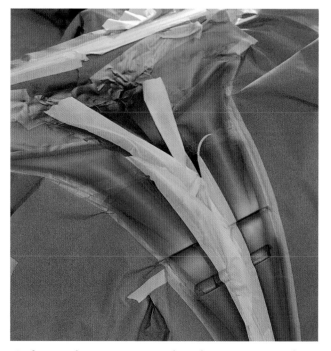

Before applying orange pearl to the outer areas Chris masks off the central V.

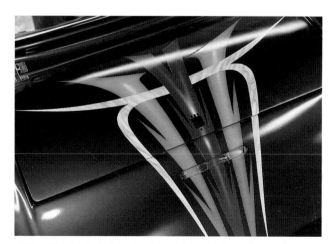

The finished airbrushed graphic, before the outlines are pinstriped.

After the graphic is finished Chris applies clearcoats, then scuffs the surface with 800 grit paper.

The first color is process blue, note how one finger is used to support and steady the hand.

Tape is used at intersections so Chris can keep the brush moving and the line consistent.

Silver is the second color. Pinstripe color is an important consideration, and a good way to enhance the design.

The red is a mix, intended to be the same hue as One-Shot bright red.

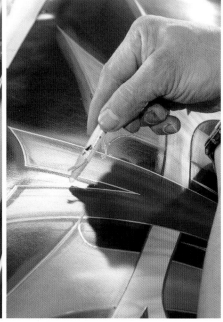

The numeral 8 is first drawn free-hand on the decklid with a china marker.

rotate the brush in the corners, explaining as he does, "When pinstripe brushes are new they're flat and they work good for long straight lines. I cut this one down so it's rounded and works better for corners."

The second color is silver from the same line of paints. Chris describes the thin lines, so consistent they look like they might have been laid down by machine, as his, "'medium lines.' I can go about half this thick, but they get so thin they don't do a good job of covering up the edge."

To make a nice red, Chris mixes roman red, orange and neon, explaining as he does, "they don't have a good bright red so I mix my own. These lines are thin and consistent and beautiful.

The finishing touch is an "8" set into the V like the old Ford V-8 symbol. The numeral is done freehand in yellow, highlighted with orange and white.

Chris has a specific process he likes to follow for clearcoating: "First the surface is cleaned with pre-cleaner then we shoot on adhesion promoter (S 64) then three coats of urethane clear (after waiting for the appropriate flash times). The clear is sanded with 800, re-cleared with two or three coats of clear, then sanded with 1500 and 2000 grit, and buffed to shine like glass."

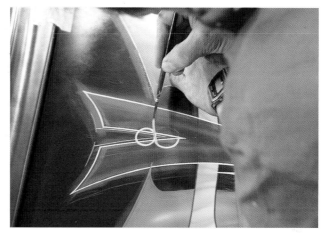

The actual color is yellow. The design is reminiscent of a Ford V-8 logo - a good choice for a '32 Ford.

Orange mid-tones and the white highlights are done with the airbrush.

The finished job is symmetrical and balanced. The graphics enhance the look of this Boss Hoss trike.

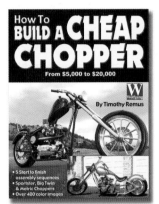

HOW TO BUILD A CHEAP CHOPPER

Choppers don't have to cost $30,000.00. In fact, a chopper built at home can be had for as little as $5,000.00. Watch the construction of 4 inexpensive choppers with complete start-to-finish photo sequences. Least expensive are metric choppers, based on a 1970s vintage Japanese four-cylinder drivetrain installed in an hardtail frame. Next up are three bikes built using Buell/Sportster drivetrains. The fact is, a complete used Buell or Sportster is an inexpensive motorcycle – and comes with wheels and tires, transmission, brakes and all the rest. Just add a hardtail frame and accessories to suit. Most expensive is bike number 4. This big-twin chopper uses a RevTech drivetrain set in a Rolling Thunder frame. Written by Tim Remus. Shot in the shops of Brian Klock, Motorcycle Works, Redneck Engineering and Dave Perewitz this book uses numerous photos to Illustrate the construction of these 4 bikes.

Eleven Chapters   144 Pages $24.95   Over 400 photos-100% color

HOW TO BUILD A CHOPPER

Designed to help you build your own chopper, this book covers History, Frames, Chassis Components, Wheels and Tires, Engine Options, Drivetrains, Wiring, Sheet Metal and Hardware. Included are assembly sequences from the Arlen Ness, Donnie Smith and American Thunder shops. Your best first step! Order today.

Choppers are back! Learn from the best how to build yours.
12 chapters cover:
- Use of Evo, TC, Shovel, Pan or Knucklehead engines
- Frame and running gear choices
- Design decisions - short and stubby or long and radical?
- Four, five or six-speed trannies

Twelve Chapters   144 Pages $24.95   Over 300 photos-over 50% color

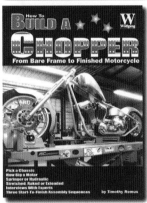

HOP-UP & CUSTOMIZE YOUR H-D BAGGER

Baggers don't have to be slow, and they don't have to look like every other Dresser in the parking lot. Take your Bagger from slow to show with a few more cubic inches, a little paint and some well placed accessories.
Whether you're looking for additional power or more visual pizazz, the answers and ideas you need are contained in this new book from Tim Remus.

Follow the project bike from start to finish, including a complete dyno test and remapping of the fuel injections. Includes two 95 inch engine make overs.
How to:
• Pick the best accessories for the best value
• Install a lowering kit
• Do custom paint on a budget
• Create a unique design for your bike

Eight Chapters   144 Pages $24.95   Over 400 full-color photos

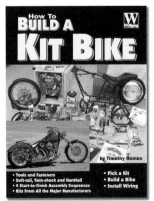

HOW TO BUILD A KIT BIKE

How To Build a Kit Bike explains how to choose the best kit and then assemble those parts into a complete running motorcycle. See bikes built in the shops of: Cory Ness, Kendall Johnson and American Thunder. If you own a kit or plan to buy a kit bike, this is the book you need — designed to help you turn that pile of parts into your own very cool motorcycle.

Eight chapters with 300+ photos & illustrations.
• Tools and Fasteners
• Soft-tail, Twin-shock and Hardtail
• 4 Start-to-Finish Assembly Sequences
• Kits From All The Major Manufacturers

Eight Chapters   144 Pages $24.95   Over 300 photos, 60% color

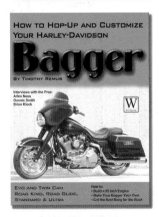

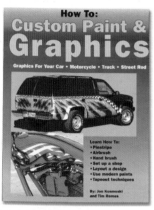

Sources

Andrew Mack and Sons
Brush Co.
225 E Chicago St.
PO Box 157
Jonesville, MI 49250
517 849 9272
www.mackbrush.com

Anderson Studios
2609 Grissom Dr.
Nashville, TN 37204
615 255 4807

Bear Air
www.bearair.com

Chris Cruz Artistry
1622 Parage Cir.
DeLand, FL 32724
386 734 3000
www.chriscruz.com

Finishline
21725 County Rd. 10
Corcoran, MN 55374
763 416 4371
www.finishlineinc.com

House of Kolor
Division of Valspar Refinish
210 Crosby St.
Picayune, MS 39466
Tech-line: 601 798 4229
www.houseofkolor.com

Krazy Kolors
Lenni Schwartz
5413 Helena
Oakdale, MN 55128
krazykolors@msn.com
www.krazykolors.net

Keith Hanson
233 Canton
Stoughton, MA 02072
781 344 9166
www.hansoncustom.net

K.C. Creations
7524 Frontage Rd.
Overland Park, KS 66204
913 642 3279

Logic Motorcycles
www.logicmotors.com
10359 W. South Range Rd.
Salem, OH 44460
330 332 2323

Matt Willoughby
9520 Youngstown-Pittburgh R.
New Middletown, OH 44442
330 542 1320

Nick Pastura
6020 W. 130th St.
Brook Park, OH 44142
216 433 1205
www.nickpastura.com

PPG
PPG.com

Steve Chaszeyka (Wizard)
11497.5 Youngstown-
Pittsburgh Rd
New Middletown, OH 44442
330 542 4444
www.wizardgraphics.us

Sid Moses Art Supplies
10456 Santa Monica Blvd.
Los Angeles, CA 90025
310 475 1111
www.moseart.com

Transfer Rite Ultra
American Biltrite Inc.
www.abitape.com

Vince Goodeve
123003 Story Book Park Rd.
RR4 Own Sound, ON
Canada N4K 5N6
goodevestudios@aol.com

X-otic paint
www.xoticcolours.com